MW01152798

WRITTEN BY
MAURICE KRAFFT,
JEAN-PIERRE VERDET,
LAURENCE OTTENHEIMER-MAQUET,
DIANE COSTA DE BEAUREGARD, MARIE FARRÉ, ANNE DE HENNING

ILLUSTRATED BY
CHRISTIAN BROUTIN, BERNARD DAGAN, LUC FAVREAU,
HENRI GALERON, DONALD GRANT, GILBERT HOUBRE,
CYRIL LEPAGNOL, JEAN-MARIE POISSENOT,
GRAHAM UNDERHILL, P. M. VALAT

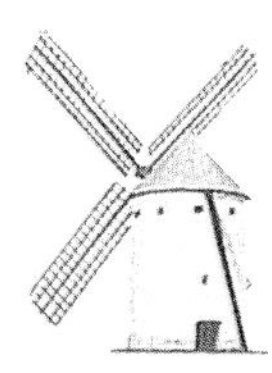

TRANSLATED AND ADAPTED BY
DR SUSANNA VAN ROSE

Dr Susanna van Rose, now a consultant geologist,
was for many years on the staff of The Geological Museum, London.

Maurice Krafft, one of the most eminent vulcanologists in the world,
died in 1991 filming the eruption of Mount Unzen in Japan.
Jean-Pierre Verdet is an astronomer at the Paris Observatory.

We gratefully acknowledge the advice of:
Christopher Hawkesworth, Professor in Earth Sciences
Dr Jane Mainwaring
Dr Anita McConnell, The Science Museum, London
Geoffrey Meaden, B.Ed., M.Sc., Ph.d.

ISBN 1 85103 128 6

Cover design by Peter Bennett
First published in Great Britain 1991 by Moonlight Publishing Ltd,
36 Stratford Road, London W8
Typeset in Great Britain by Technical Arts Services, Loughton
Printed in Italy by Editoriale Libraria

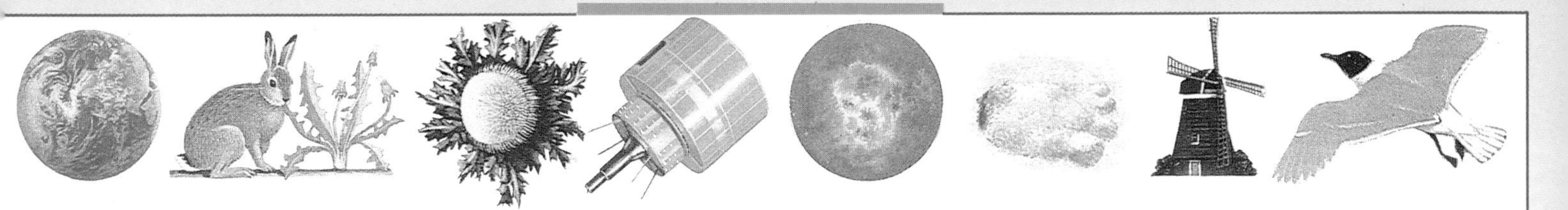

OUR PLANET EARTH

CONTENTS

MOONLIGHT PUBLISHING

The Earth circles round the Sun.

Without the Sun there would be no life on the Earth. The Sun gives out warmth and light. It makes the plants grow and you in turn depend on the plants. Without the Sun the Earth would be a barren, icy, desert. Yet the Sun is an ordinary star, only one among millions and millions. It just happens to be the star at the centre of our solar system, and the Earth is one of its several planets. In prehistoric times, people worshipped it, building special monuments to the Sun.

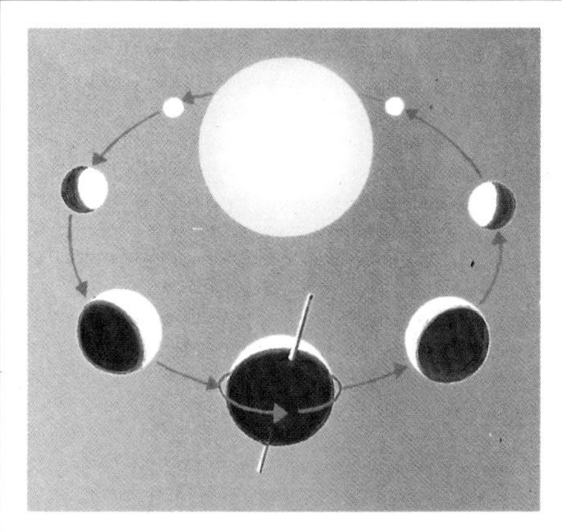

The Earth takes a year to go round the Sun. At the same time it is spinning like a top. It makes one complete turn every twenty-four hours.

It was once thought that the Earth was fixed at the centre of the Universe, and that the stars travelled around the Earth. Although to you the ground seems solid and still, the Earth is spinning and hurtling through space at high speed, carrying you with it.
The idea that the Earth revolves around the Sun was put forward by the astronomer Nicolaus Copernicus, four hundred years ago.

How does the Earth travel in space?
Every morning you see the Sun rise.
It travels across the sky, and sets each evening – in fact it is the Earth itself which is moving, not the Sun.
During the course of a whole day and night the Earth completes one spin or rotation.
In addition, over the course of one year, the Earth travels right round the Sun.

The planets of the solar system
The Earth is not the only planet turning around the Sun. Starting from the Sun, the other planets are:
Mercury (1), Venus (2), Mars (3), Jupiter (4), Saturn with its rings (5), Uranus (6), Neptune (7), and Pluto (8).
Other travelling companions are our Moon and the moons of some other planets.

The Moon, the Earth and other planets do not give off any light or heat of their own. They shine only because they reflect back light from the Sun.

The Earth is part of the Solar System.

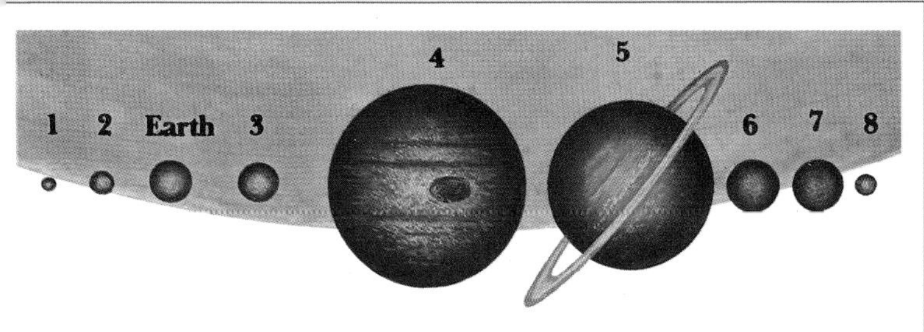

Nearest to the Sun is Mercury (1) followed by the other planets and the Earth. The picture shows the planets' sizes in relation to each other, but not the distances between them. To do that, this book would have to be over a kilometre wide!

Mercury (1), **Mars** (3) and **Pluto** (8) are small like the Earth, and have a solid rocky surface. **Jupiter** (4), **Saturn** (5), **Uranus** (6) and **Neptune** (7) are huge, and are surrounded by a thick atmosphere of gas. Other space travellers, much smaller than the planets, are comets and meteorites. **Meteorites** come from the many small fragments which are crowded between Mars and Jupiter. They may be part of a planet which has broken apart.

The Sun is a million times larger than the Earth. But the Sun is only a small star compared with other stars in the Universe.

Venus (2) is about the same size as the Earth, but with a temperature of up to 500 degrees Celsius it is far too hot for there to be any life. The Earth, further away from the Sun, has a more comfortable temperature.
Venus is known as the morning star and the evening star. At dawn, when the stars fade, Venus shines for a little longer.
At nightfall, it is the first, with Mercury, to appear.

The rings of Saturn are not solid; they are made up of many icy fragments. Each is a tiny satellite travelling around Saturn itself. The two outer rings, furthest from Saturn, are the most brilliant. Next comes a ring which is not so bright, and is less crowded with fragments, then the fourth, the innermost ring of all, which is the least bright.

The Moon, the Earth's companion in space

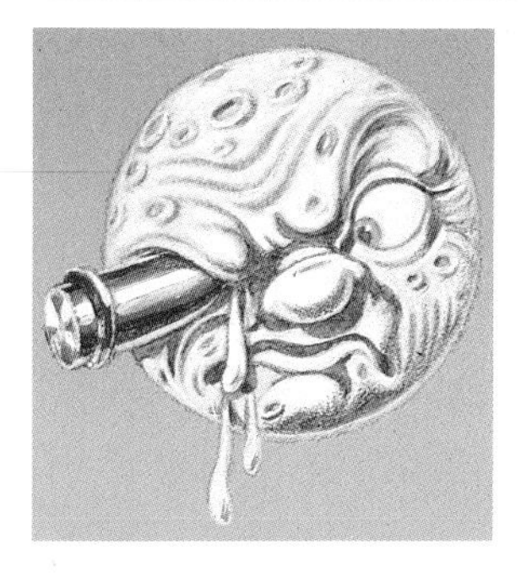

Throughout the ages people have been fascinated by the Moon.
Some have seen a human or animal face in the patterns on its surface.
If you promise somebody the Moon you are promising something quite impossible . . . And it always seemed impossible that men should actually walk on the Moon . . . until one day in 1969 when the American astronaut Neil Armstrong stepped out of his spaceship on to that dry and dusty surface.

The Moon is small. Its diameter is only about a quarter the diameter of the Earth.

The Moon and the Earth are the same age.

In 1969 two American astronauts, Neil Armstrong and Buzz Aldrin, landed on the Moon in Apollo 11, a special lunar craft. They brought back to the Earth the first samples of lunar soil for scientific examination.

The Moon has been bombarded by meteorites over thousands of millions of years, making the pits called craters on its surface. Moon rocks brought back by the astronauts have been tested by scientists and the results show that the Moon and the Earth had a common origin. They are both about 4650 million years old. Moon rocks turned out to be very much like some of the rocks on Earth.

The Moon only shines because it reflects back the light which falls on it from the Sun.

At full Moon, you can see dark markings on the Moon's surface – the lunar seas or maria. In fact there is no water on the Moon; the maria are vast plains covered with a dark-coloured dust. The pale marks are the lunar mountains, the tallest being 8,000 metres high.

If you look at the Moon with a pair of good binoculars, you will be able to see these mountains and the pits of all sizes which cover the Moon, as well as ravines and valleys.

Photographs taken from spaceships show us the other, hidden, face of the Moon. This is invisible from the Earth. In the time the Moon spins once, it also makes one full journey around the Earth, so it always points the same face towards us.

At full Moon it is light enough to see at night.

The Earth and the Moon play hide and seek.

The Moon travels round the Earth and if the Moon shone with its own light, we would be able to see it all the time. However, because the Moon and the Earth are both lit by the Sun, what we see of the Moon depends on its position in relation to the Earth and the Sun. These regular changes in the way the Moon looks in the sky are called the phases of the Moon.

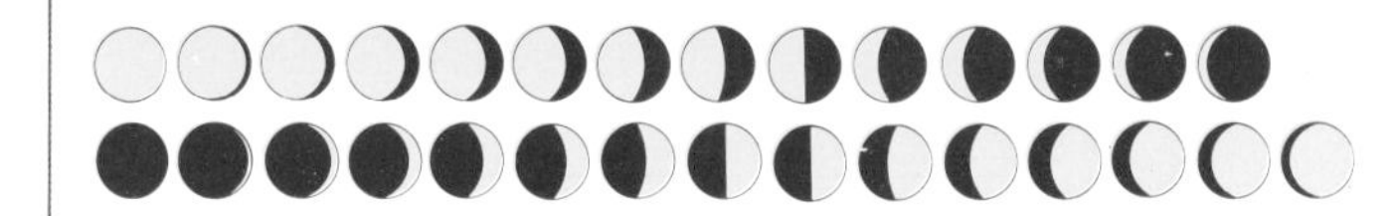

These are the phases the Moon goes through in 27.3 days, which is one lunar month. So a lunar month is a little bit shorter than a calendar month.

The new Moon appears in the sky as a thin crescent. It grows wider, from quarter, to half, to full circle – called full Moon. Then, night by night, it becomes smaller and thinner again.

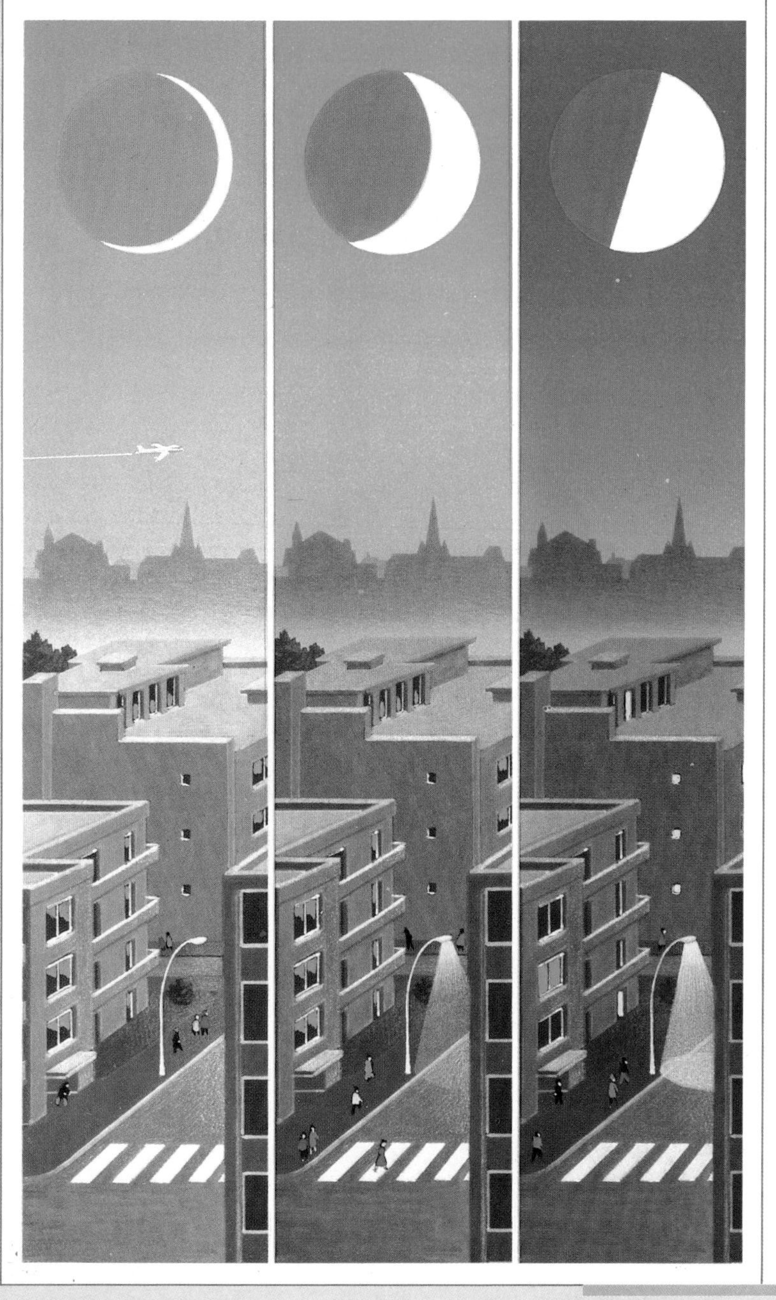

The Moon waxes and wanes each month.

At the time of new Moon, the Moon is between the Sun and the Earth. The side being lit by the Sun is facing away from the Earth, and we see none of it.
The thin crescent of the new Moon is the very edge of the sunlit side. Days later, the Moon's position has changed and we can see more of its lit face. Full Moon occurs when the Moon is on the opposite side of the Earth from the Sun.
The Moon sets as the Sun rises.

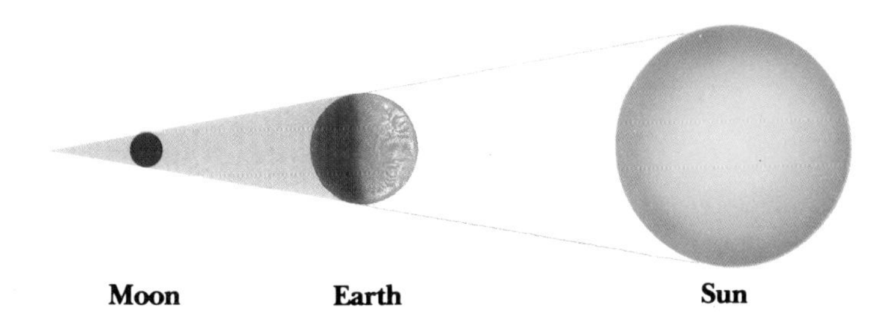

The positions of the Moon, the Earth and the Sun at the time of an eclipse of the Moon.

Eventually the Moon can be seen as a pale half Moon in the morning sky. The part lit by the Sun becomes smaller and smaller until it is just a thin sliver. Then it is the beginning of the lunar month and in a few days the Moon again appears as a crescent in the evening sky.
The weeks and months of our calendar are calculated from the phases of the Moon.

The Moon slowly moves into the Earth's shadow. At full eclipse, the Moon disappears altogether for a few moments.

Eclipses of the Moon

Just like you do, the Moon and the Earth cast shadows. Sometimes in their age-long game of hide-and-seek, the Moon passes through the Earth's shadow, causing what we call an eclipse.
At first only a small part of the Moon is in shadow, but in a few minutes it is all in darkness. There is usually one eclipse of the Moon each year.

Sometimes strange shining lights flash across the sky.

The pattern of the night sky is disturbed by the flash of a comet. A comet is a fireball with a long, shining tail of gas. Comets come from far away in the solar system, and we see them when, occasionally, they pass near the Sun.

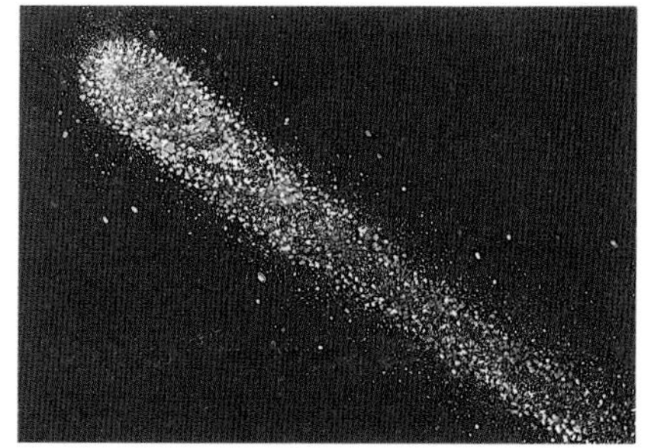

Halley's Comet and its brilliant tail of luminous dust and gas. The tail is only lit up as the comet gets close to the Sun.

In times gone by, people were terrified of comets. However, the Earth has passed through the tails of comets many times without coming to any harm.

In 1758 a comet passed across the skies. It was given the name Halley's comet in honour of the astronomer Edmund Halley who had predicted its appearance in 1705.

Meteorites – pennies from heaven

Some artificial satellites have solar paddles which turn the Sun's energy into electricity to power their instruments.

The machines we send out into space to orbit the Earth are artificial satellites. They may be used for military purposes, for communications, such as satellite television, or to monitor the weather.

Have you ever seen shooting stars?

These are meteorites, many only as large as a grain of sand. Sometimes one passes close to the Earth, and is pulled into the Earth's atmosphere. It travels fast, and gets very hot, so hot that in contact with the air it turns into gas. This hot gas shines like a bright trail across the sky.

In 1900, a meteorite this size tore out a track 60 kilometres wide through the forest of Siberia.

Most meteorites burn up completely and only the largest ever land on Earth. The biggest known weighed 36 tonnes.

Meteor Crater, Arizona, in the USA, is 1,200 metres across. It was hollowed out by a giant meteorite.

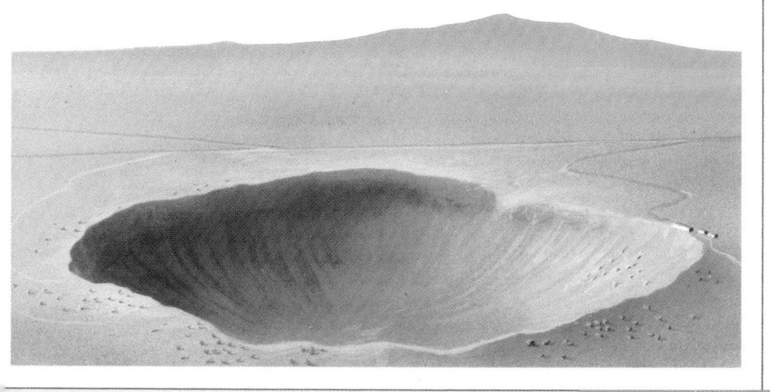

The birth of the stars

What can you see, when you look into the sky on a clear night?

About 2,500 stars! Some of the lights you see are actually made up of pairs of stars, so there are even more than you could count.

Stars are being born every minute somewhere in the Universe.

Often stars are born in clusters, from huge clouds of hydrogen. A powerful telescope shows stars being born in the Trifid Nebula.

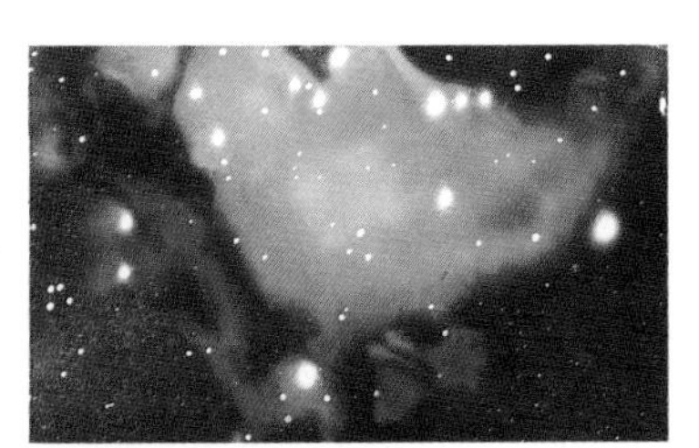

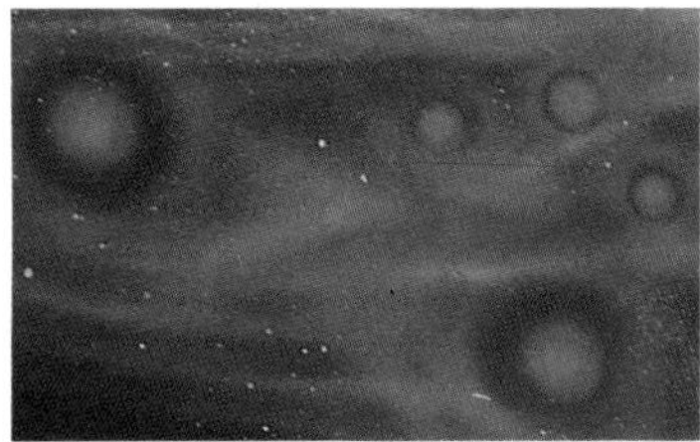

A cloud of gas and dust starts to collapse. As this happens, a star begins to take shape.

The more the cloud collapses, the hotter the gas becomes. Eventually the gas is so hot it starts to shine with light; a star is born.

When the star has burned its hydrogen, it grows into a red giant, and then shrinks to a white dwarf.

How do stars live and die?

Stars are enormous gas balls, which are very, very hot. They are so hot they shine brightly, and in a very special way. They shine by transforming their hydrogen into another gas, helium. The change gives out light energy, and may go on for millions of years.

Eventually though, stars burn out.

If they are very large stars, they explode. The small ones become very cold. Our star, the Sun, is a medium-sized star, neither especially large nor especially small.

Constellations you can see in the sky in summer in the northern hemisphere if you are looking south:

1. The Lyre
2. Hercules
3. Ophiuchus
4. The Northern Crown
5. The Charioteer
6. The Virgin
7. The Scales
8. The Archer
9. The Sea Goat
10. The Water-bearer
11. The Fishes
12. Pegasus
13. The Dolphin
14. Aquila
15. The Swan
16. The Serpent
17. The Scorpion

The stars in the night sky are a map for travellers.

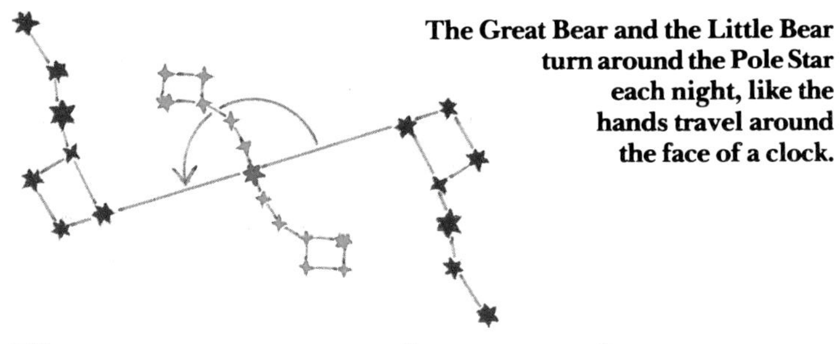

The Great Bear and the Little Bear turn around the Pole Star each night, like the hands travel around the face of a clock.

The stars seem to us to be arranged in patterns across the sky

These are the constellations. Like you, they have their own names. The Great Bear, made up of seven stars, is sometimes seen as the shape of a saucepan. The side of the pan points towards the Pole Star, which is about five times as far away as the height of the pan itself. The Pole Star is the fixed point in the sky around which all the other stars seem to turn. The Pole Star tells travellers where north is.

If you look at the sky in the northern hemisphere in winter, facing north, these are some of the constellations you can look for:

1. Orion
2. The Bull
3. The Pleiades
4. Perseus
5. The Ram
6. The Charioteer
7. Andromeda
8. Pegasus
9. The Fishes
10. The Water-bearer
11. The Whale
12. Eridanus

During the year, the Earth passes through the twelve constellations of the Zodiac. Astrologers believe these constellations have influence over our lives . . .

The twelve constellations of the Zodiac are:

The Twins	**The Fishes**	**The Archer**	**The Virgin**
The Bull	**The Water-bearer**	**The Scorpion**	**The Lion**
The Ram	**The Sea Goat**	**The Scales**	**The Crab**

Our very own star, the Sun

It was once thought that the Sun was a huge fireball burning in the sky like a great lump of coal. Even such an enormous lump of coal would have burned out after only 7,000 years! The Sun has been shining much much longer than that.
Like all the other stars, the Sun is a giant ball of very hot gas. Its surface burns at 4,300 degrees Celsius. Inside, at the centre, it's even hotter. The temperature reaches 10,000,000 degrees.

This drawing shows how people thought the Sun looked, 400 years ago. Below, you can see how the Sun really looks when viewed through a telescope.

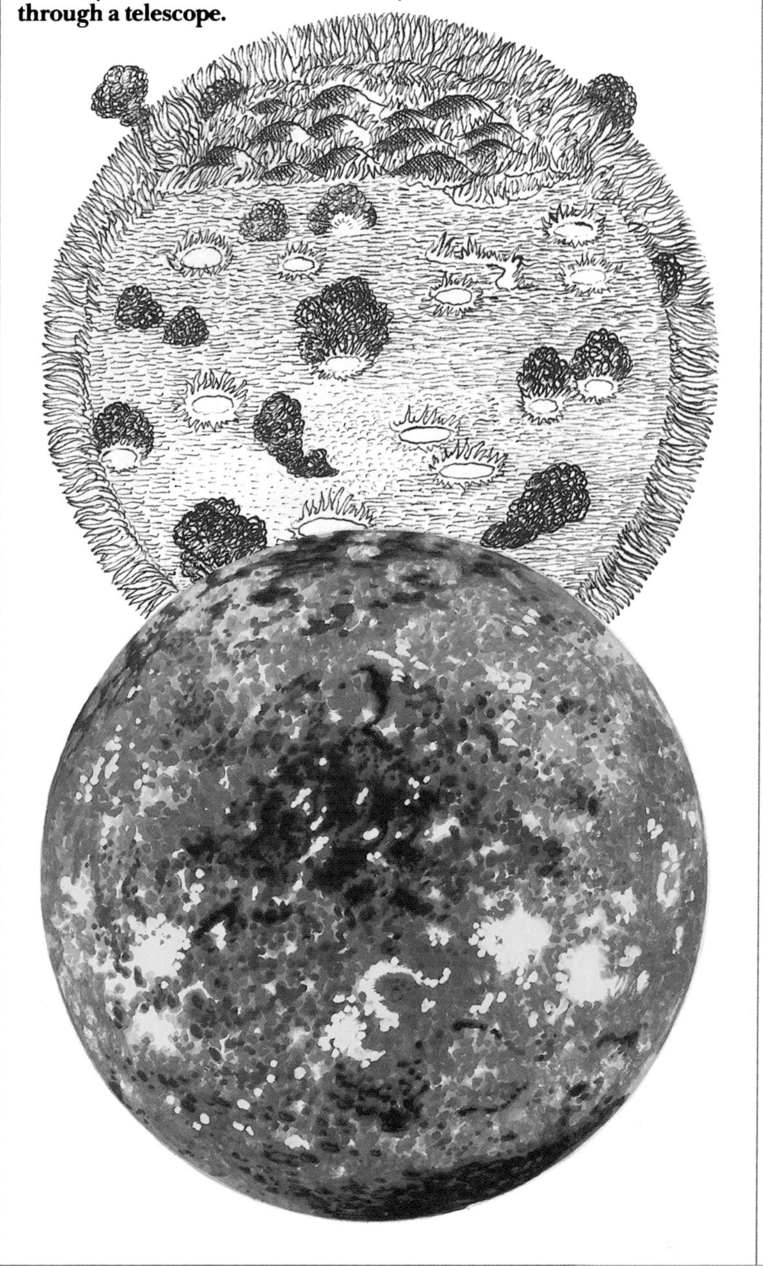

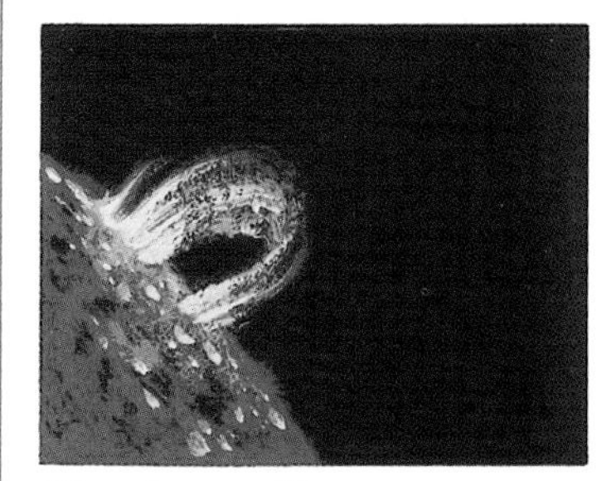

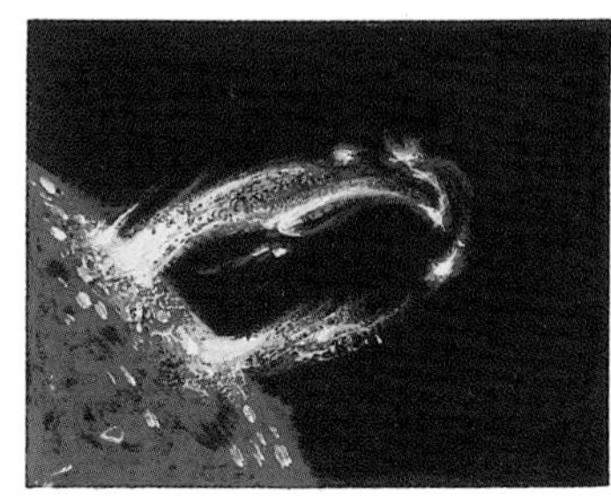

Giant loops of hot gas are now and then thrown off from the boiling surface of the Sun: these are solar flares.

The Sun is an enormous source of energy.
It is a huge hydrogen bomb, which has been exploding for the last five million years, and giving out energy. Scientists expect it will carry on for another five million years. If you imagine the Sun as a person, it would be middle-aged. When the Sun has used up all its hydrogen energy, it will become a cold dwarf star, and will no longer shine.

Now the Sun shines continuously.
Some of the Sun's energy hits the Earth, it warms us and the plants and animals that live here. The Sun is far enough away for its heat to warm us without burning us up. The Sun's energy also reaches us as light: this is very powerful, strong enough to burn your eyes, so never stare directly at the Sun.

The Sun gives out energy even when we cannot see it through thick clouds or fog. These only block a little of the light and warmth and although it may seem cold to us, it is nothing compared to the cold we would feel if the Sun no longer existed.

The Sun hides behind the Moon in a solar eclipse.

How can the Moon hide the Sun?

It seems impossible as the Moon is much smaller than the Sun. But because it is so much closer to the Earth it looks the same size. The Earth takes a year to travel all the way round the Sun, but the Moon goes round the Earth in one month. About once a year, the Moon passes directly in front of the Sun, hiding it from us. It becomes as dark as night in daytime. This is an eclipse of the Sun.

On parts of the Earth which are directly in line with the Sun and the Moon, the effect of the eclipse will look like the picture on the right.

In Britain, the last total eclipse happened in 1927. The next will be in 1999.

Myriads of stars make up the Milky Way, the galaxy we live in.

Our galaxy, the Milky Way, looks like this from the side.

The Sun and the solar system are only a small part of one galaxy in the Universe. Our galaxy alone contains 100 thousand million stars.

Our galaxy is called the Milky Way.

On a clear moonless night, the Milky Way looks like a hazy silvery band, but if you look at it through binoculars you will see it is made up of many stars. It has arms which float out in delicate spirals from a centre. From the side it looks like a giant flattened wheel. The Milky Way is rotating, carrying us with it, in a journey around the Universe. Each spin takes 250 thousand million years.

If we could travel beyond our galaxy and look straight at it, it would look rather like the spiral galaxy in the picture.
Not all galaxies are spiral in shape like ours. Others look like elliptical, or oval-shaped blobs of light.
All contain thousands of millions of stars.

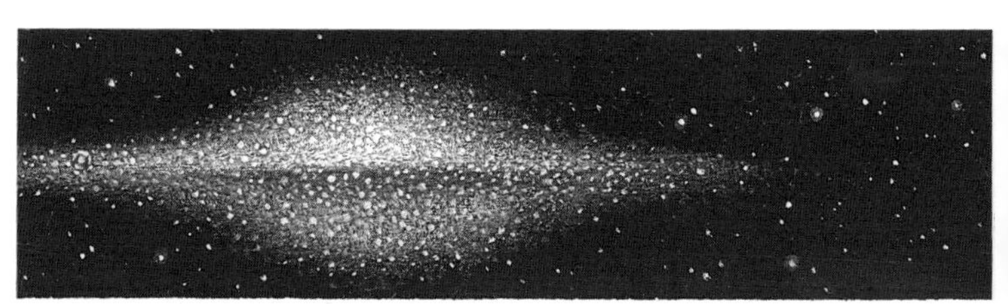

The Milky Way. The small red spot shows where the Sun and our solar system are within it.

There are other areas of misty light in the night sky which are difficult to make out. They are called nebulae – which means indistinct and hazy. Some are galaxies and star systems. Others are huge clouds of gas and dust, like the Trifid Nebula.
They shine when a star lights them.

The Universe contains millions and millions of galaxies.

Although our galaxy seems huge to us, it is small compared to others, such as our near neighbour Andromeda.

The Milky Way is like an island, one among millions in the Universe.

The Earth and the Sun are right out on the edge of the Milky Way, our galaxy.

The Earth's only natural satellite is the Moon, but many artificial satellites now orbit, or go round, the Earth too. Once launched, these satellites (such as the International Ultraviolet Explorer) stay in orbit. Gravity is the force that holds us and everything around us on the Earth; it also keeps the Moon and all the other satellites in orbit. Advances in technology have brought more and more powerful telescopes, so that astronomers can see stars which were invisible before. There are even telescopes, like the new Hubble Space Telescope, looking at the stars from satellites orbiting the Earth!

The largest optical telescope in the world is in Georgia, in the USSR.

The Sun's daily journey across the sky

Day follows night, winter follows summer, and the years come and go in an endless succession. Our whole solar system is regulated by the movements of the planets.

Humans and other animals are used to the way the solar system works. After a day, we need rest and sleep, which we usually take at night. These changes govern the rhythm of our daily lives, and without this rhythm, life would be exhausting.

The Sun rises each day in the east.

The Sun looks as though it follows a great curve across the sky each day.
In the mornings the Sun rises in the east and, until midday, it climbs ever higher in the sky. Then it begins to drop until, at the end of the day, it sets in the west. As the Sun disappears, the sky grows darker and it becomes night.

Actually the Sun isn't moving at all: it is the Earth which is moving.
Since the Earth is round, only one side at a time is lit by the Sun. The half of the Earth which faces the Sun has day, while on the other side, it is night.
The Earth itself is turning around, so all parts are lit by the Sun's light in turn. When the Sun sets on you, your home passes from day into night, and from light into darkness, as it moves out of the Sun's light into the shadowed side of the Earth. When the Sun rises again, your home moves out of the darkness, into the warm light of the Sun once more. It is not the Sun which moves, it is the Earth, and it carries all of us living creatures with it.

The Earth turns once every twenty-four hours.
This length of time is called a day.

Different countries on Earth have different clock times. At breakfast time in Britain, it is evening in America. Britain's evening corresponds to early morning in Japan.

Day follows night and night follows day.

The four seasons . . .

It is spring. At the spring equinox, the Sun takes twelve hours to cross the sky from dawn to dusk. Then every morning as we tilt towards the Sun it rises earlier and sets later in the evenings. As the days get longer so more warmth and light fall on our side of the Earth each day.

It is summer. The days are long. In Britain they last about sixteen hours.
In the northern hemisphere, 21 June is the longest day of the year: it is called the summer solstice.

The Earth is tipped at an angle in its path round the Sun, so each day of the year you see the Sun make a slightly different journey across the sky.

The Earth makes an immense journey around the Sun – about 1,000 million kilometres each year.

As the Earth travels round the Sun we pass through different seasons.
The Earth's surface is curved, so the Sun's rays spread out when they reach it. In summer our part of the Earth is tilted towards the Sun so the rays are more direct and it is hotter. In winter we are tilted away from the Sun and it is summer on the other side of the Earth.

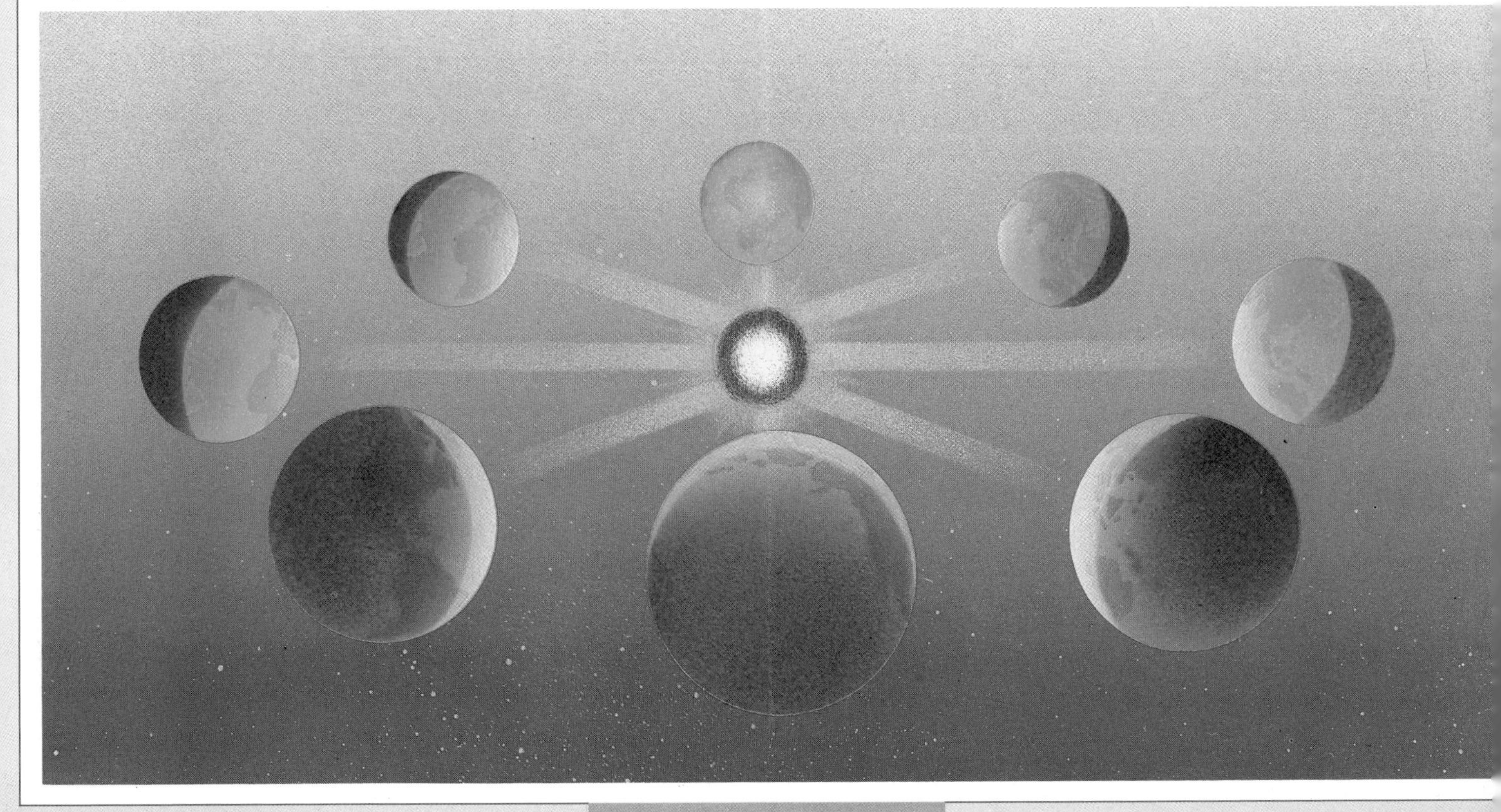

At midday, the Sun reaches its highest point in the sky. From the summer solstice onwards, the days get shorter.

It is autumn. At the autumn equinox, day and night are once again the same length. Then each day the Sun rises later and each evening night arrives earlier. The Sun's light falls ever more at an angle and the air grows colder.

It is winter. It is dark before four o'clock. The shortest day of the year is the winter solstice, just before Christmas.

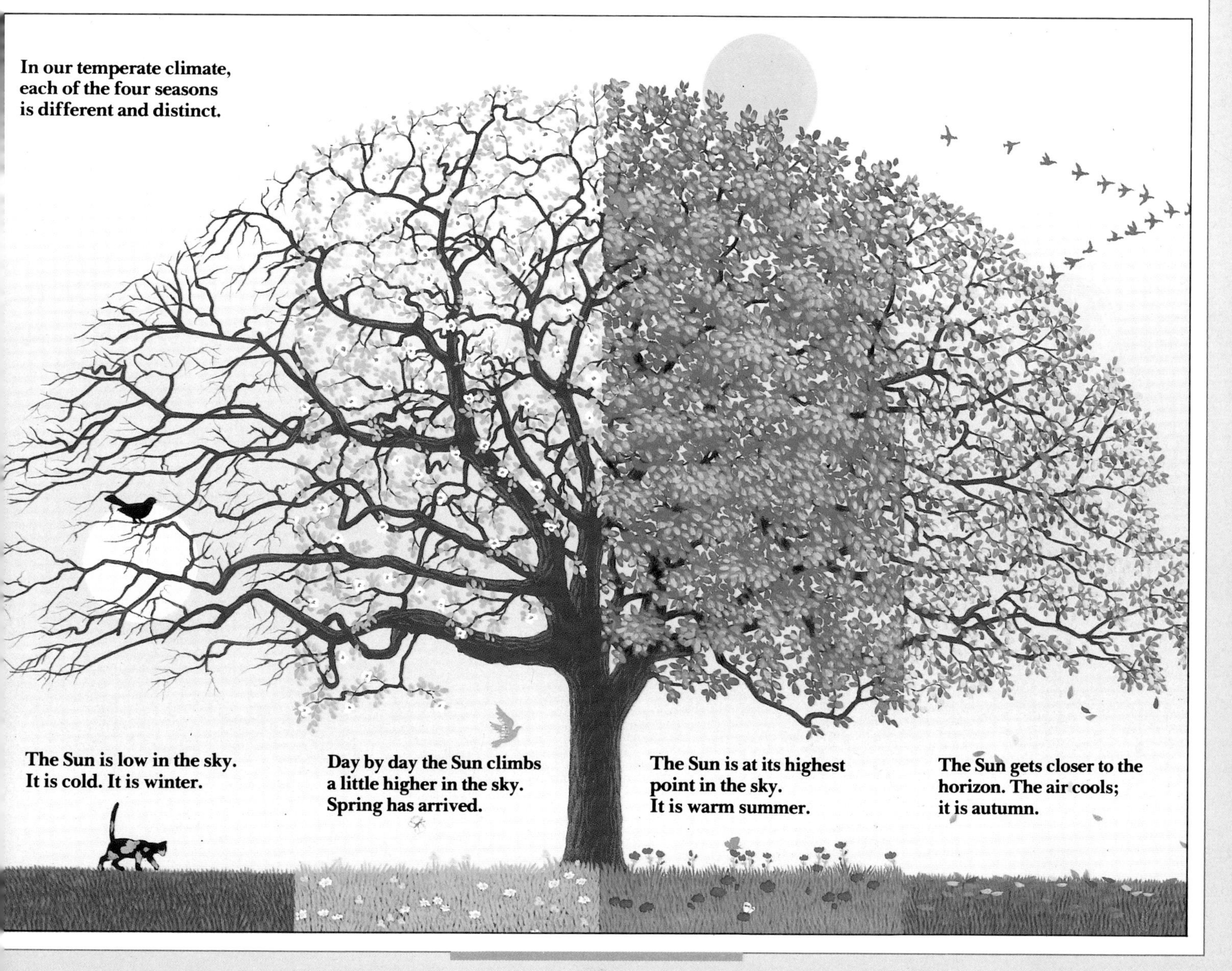

In our temperate climate, each of the four seasons is different and distinct.

The Sun is low in the sky. It is cold. It is winter.

Day by day the Sun climbs a little higher in the sky. Spring has arrived.

The Sun is at its highest point in the sky. It is warm summer.

The Sun gets closer to the horizon. The air cools; it is autumn.

The seasons at the Poles and the Equator

The Sun's light and heat fall unequally on the Earth.
Near the Equator, the changes in the seasons and in the length of the day are different from those in Europe.
The Equator is never tilted away from the Sun. If you lived there you would see the Sun pass directly overhead at midday. You would then have no shadow because the light falls vertically on you! Here, night and day are almost the same length and it is hot all the year round.
The Poles are never tilted towards the Sun, so the Sun is low in the sky. Its rays slant down, passing through a greater amount of atmosphere and so losing their heat. This is why it's cold all year round. Night lasts for six months and neither heat nor light arrive from the Sun during that time.

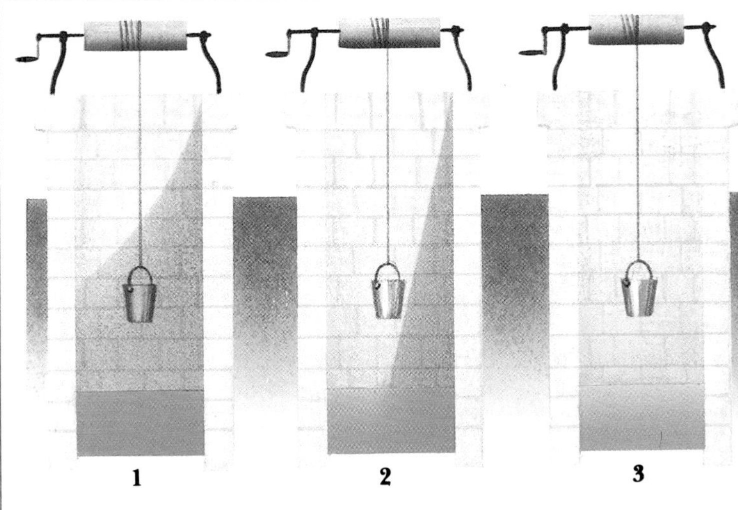

See how the Sun's rays fall at midday in a deep well; in northern Norway (1), in southern England (2), and at the Equator (3), where even the deepest well is lit right to the bottom.

Then comes the summer when it is always light. Day lasts six months, the Sun never sets, and you can see it shining in the sky at midnight.

The North and South Poles have opposite seasons. When the North Pole is basking in the midnight Sun that never sets, the South Pole has its period of long winter darkness.

The polar night sky is lit up by multicoloured veils.

The polar aurora
sometimes lights up the skies of the Arctic and of Antarctica with a wonderful spectacle of multicoloured veils.

A fairytale scene
In the north, in the Arctic, this is called the aurora borealis, and in the south, in Antarctica, it is the aurora australis. Green, purple and gold, they appear like shimmering curtains, or giant coloured waterfalls, depending on where in the sky they hang. These splendid light displays come from the Sun, which occasionally gives out a flood of charged particles, the solar wind. The charged particles are trapped by the Earth's magnetism at the Poles, where they shine brightly to create these beautiful effects.

The Earth's climate is very varied.
In Britain we live half-way between the cold, dry North Pole and the baking hot, humid Equator. The Poles are **freezing deserts,** where ice and snow cover the sea and the land all year round. There are few animals or plants and the temperature may fall below minus 50 degrees Celsius.
The parched deserts of the great continents are large regions where no rain falls for years at a time. Rain clouds cannot develop because the ground and air are so dry. The land is scorched by day and chilled at night so few plants and animals can live here.

The rain forests, are nourished by the long wet seasons, and torrential downpours of rain every day of the year. Dense leafy trees grow tall above luxuriant shrubs and undergrowth. Many different plants and animals live in the rain forests.

Western Europe has **a temperate climate** with rain falling most of the year and no fierce extremes of temperature. The rivers rarely run dry. Outdoor temperatures are neither especially hot nor cold. Many different kinds of plants and animals can live here, in the ever-changing four seasons.

A cloak of air surrounds the Earth.

It may seem as if the air is impossible to see or feel... but in fact it is all around us. It blows against you when it's windy and sweeps the clouds across the sky. You can't see it but you can see what it does. And even though you can't see it, it is extremely important to us.
You need air to breathe, even when you're asleep. It contains vital oxygen without which you would die.

Run very fast with your arms and hands stretched out wide – feel the air pushing against you.

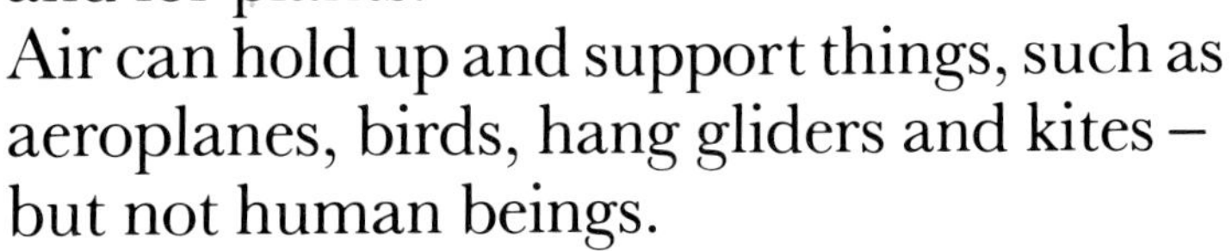

The air surrounds us all.
The air is a mixture of gases such as nitrogen, oxygen and carbon dioxide which are necessary for us and for plants.
Air can hold up and support things, such as aeroplanes, birds, hang gliders and kites – but not human beings.

The layer of air which surrounds the Earth is called the atmosphere.
Down at the level of the sea, the atmosphere is at its thickest. We feel the whole weight of it – this is atmospheric pressure. Because it is there all the time, we forget about it. But 6,000 metres up, atmospheric pressure has only half the sea-level value. Pressure becomes less and less at ever greater heights, till in space it is zero. This is a vacuum. Astronauts in spaceships travel through this nothingness. If they left the artificial atmosphere of the ship without special suits on, their bodies would explode.
Oxygen is essential to life. Mountain climbers use oxygen masks on very high mountains. Without it, they would not be able to sleep, keep warm, and climb.

The atmosphere is a filter which protects us from the Sun.
The Sun gives out an enormous amount of heat and light, but most bounces off the Earth's atmosphere.

Air makes the sky blue, and controls the temperature on Earth.

The rest penetrates into the Earth's atmosphere and heats up the surface. Fortunately, during the night, much of this ground heat escapes again. If it didn't, the ground would become so hot, the oceans and seas would boil.

The atmosphere also acts like a huge glass roof. By day it filters the Sun's rays. By night it insulates, holding in some of the heat, so the Earth does not cool down too much.

In high mountains, where the atmosphere is thin, the temperatures vary enormously between day and night.

The air scatters the light from the Sun. Without air, the Sun and the stars would shine at midday on a totally black background of sky. Dust and water drops in the air absorb light, and give the sky its blue and sunset colours.

1. The Sun rises. Today the air is damp, and sunbeams are reflected off the water in the air giving a white light.

2. During the day the sky changes colour.

3. On a fine day, as the Sun rises, the air gets drier and clearer. The sky becomes a bright blue.

4. It is the sunlight scattered by the gas and water in the air which gives the sky its different colours.

5. At sunset, the Sun's light travels through the dusty, lower levels of the atmosphere. The sky shines red.

6. Once the Sun has set, its rays no longer light up the air, and the sky becomes dark.

The wind is a great, flowing current of air.

Force 0: total calm

Force 3: gentle breeze

Force 6: fresh wind

Force 8: gale

The air around us is always moving. This movement is called turbulence.

A tree distorted by the wind.

As the air moves, so it creates the wind.

Why is the air always moving?

Warm air rises because it is lighter in weight than cold air. This causes movement and wind. At the seaside, for example, the cold air over the sea moves down to replace the warm air which is rising over the beach; a sea breeze blows on to the land.

Air currents on the Earth, seen from space.

At ground level the air may be quite calm. When smoke rises straight up into the sky, there is no wind in the air. Even so, higher up, the clouds may be moving, and there is wind.

At very high altitude, around 12 kilometres up, strong air currents encircle the Earth. Aircraft use these to speed up their journeys.

Windmills use the power of the wind to turn their sails.

Force 10: storm

Force 12: hurricane

Measuring the strength of the wind

The force of the wind is measured from 0 to 12. Force 0 corresponds to absolute calm, and force 12 to a hurricane, when the wind speed is more than 120 kilometres an hour. It was Admiral Beaufort, a British Admiral born in 1774, who first thought of this way of measuring the wind, so the scale is called the Beaufort scale after him.

Storms in Western Europe don't as a rule get stronger than force 10. Hurricanes at force 12 normally only happen in the parts of the Earth closer to the Equator.

At the North and South Poles, stormy blizzards blow in violent gusts. They sometimes begin quite suddenly. The wind may blow faster than 15 metres a second. The snow is whipped along with it, and you cannot even see as far as your hand.

A wind vane can be used to produce electricity when the wind turns its blades.

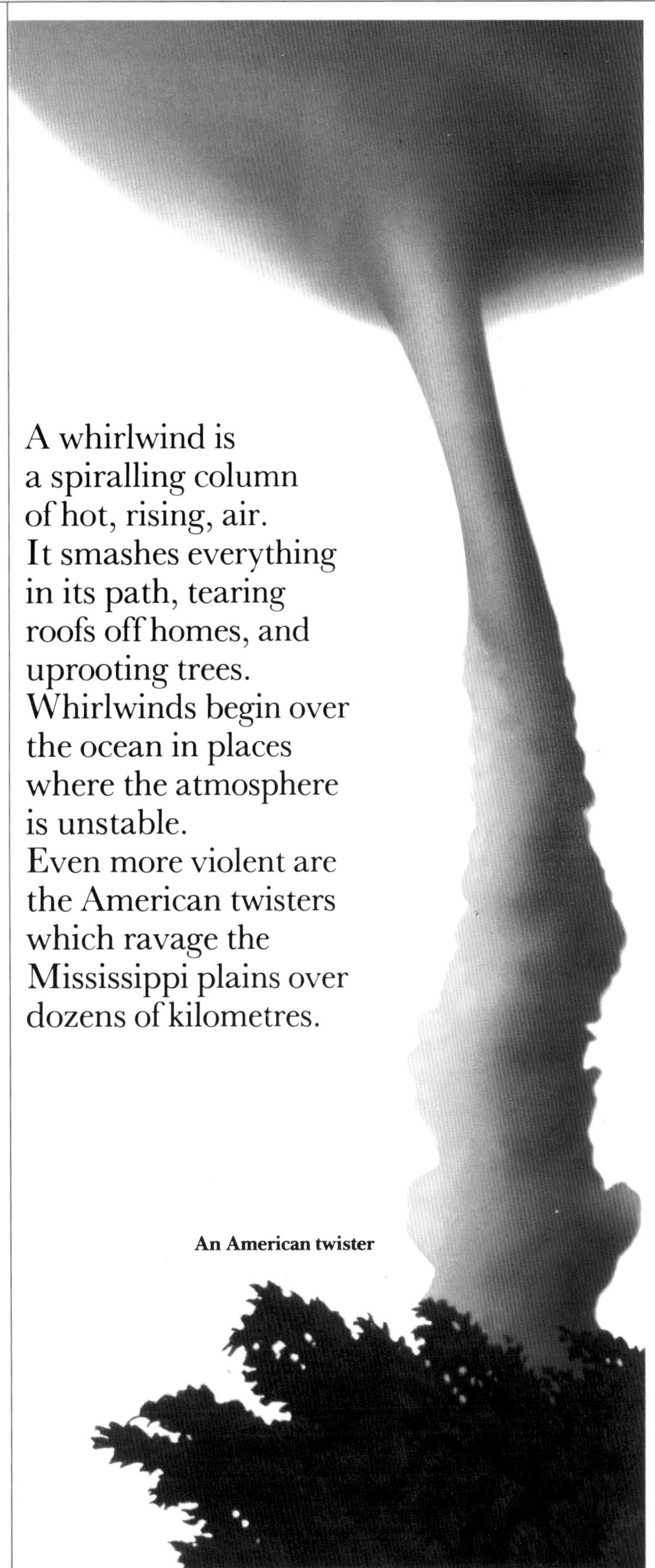

A whirlwind is a spiralling column of hot, rising, air. It smashes everything in its path, tearing roofs off homes, and uprooting trees. Whirlwinds begin over the ocean in places where the atmosphere is unstable. Even more violent are the American twisters which ravage the Mississippi plains over dozens of kilometres.

An American twister

As the clouds grow, it rains.

An old proverb says: rain before seven, fine before eleven. In our climate, the weather changes often. Early morning rain can be followed by a fine afternoon, and then by evening black rain clouds may be gathering on the horizon.

Where do clouds come from?
There is water in the air, in rivers and canals, on snow-covered mountains and above all in the seas and oceans. More than three-quarters of the Earth's surface is covered with water. The heat of the Sun transforms the water into vapour, which rises and collects into clouds as it cools. Cold air cannot hold as much water vapour as warm air, so the vapour becomes liquid once again and it begins to rain.

The water cycle.
Rainwater goes into rivers and then to the sea. There the water evaporates, forms clouds, and falls again as rain. The Earth's water is never lost.

Clouds make landscapes in the sky.

You can try this yourself, but be careful: steam burns! Put a cold plate over the spout of a boiling kettle; the underside of the plate will get covered with water! When it meets the cold plate, the water vapour becomes liquid again. It condenses. In the sky, clouds are made of tiny drops of water which join up to make bigger drops.

Why do raindrops fall from the clouds?
There are millions of tonnes of water floating around as clouds above your head. Not all clouds will produce rain. The drops only fall if they grow big enough. Little drops collect together to become big drops, till eventually they are too heavy to float in the clouds. Then they fall as rain.

What kinds of clouds are there?
There are many different kinds of clouds, so if you know what to look for it is always interesting to gaze up at the sky. Some clouds are very tall, and shaped like enormous cauliflowers; these are the white fluffy cumulus clouds. Generally they mean fine weather. Sometimes, though, they grow very large, and look like mushrooms at the top. This means there will be a thunderstorm.

Other clouds are more horizontal in shape, in thin layers: these are stratus clouds.

Cirrus clouds are more like snowflakes. They are thin and feathery, and may even look as though they have been drawn out as threads. When they are about 2,500 metres up they are called strato-cirrus. Higher, between 2,000 and 6,000 metres up, they are alto-cirrus. Cirro-stratus look like a thin mist and sometimes make the Sun or Moon appear to have a coloured halo.

Alto-cumulus hover around 4,000 metres up and look like big blotches – they make the sky dappled.

So look up into the sky and watch these wonderful cloudscapes as they pass overhead.

1. Cirro-stratus
2. Alto-cumulus
3. Cumulo-nimbus
4. Cumulus

Lightning strikes, thunder rumbles. It's a thunderstorm!

On a really hot day the air rises very high very fast. Huge cumulo-nimbus form and the horizon grows black.
The wind gets stronger: a storm is brewing. Inside the clouds, water drops are swirling around. This rush of movement creates electricity and sparks of lightning leap out of the clouds. The sound of thunder rolls across the sky. Quick, it's time to get home!

The Greek god Zeus throwing thunderbolts across the sky

Zig-zags of light shoot between two clouds, or between the clouds and the ground. This is lightning!

Lightning is terrifying and can be dangerous. It takes the fastest way it can to get to the ground, running down anything high – a church steeple, a tree, a pointed rock, an umbrella or even water.

On some buildings you will see a lightning conductor, an aerial which leads the electricity in the lightning straight into the ground.

Lightning also makes a great deal of noise. This is **thunder** .

Even when the thunderstorm is far away, you can see the lightning immediately: the light travels fast – at 300,000 kilometres a second. The sound of thunder takes longer to arrive.
Sound only travels at 330 metres a second. So it may be several seconds after you see the lightning that you hear its thunder.
To work out how far away a storm is, count the seconds and multiply by the speed of sound (330 metres per second). If you count ten seconds, the storm is 3,300 metres away – 3.3 kilometres away from you.

During a thunderstorm, never shelter under a tree. You are safest at home.

A rainbow is a bridge of coloured light across the sky.

Sometimes after a shower of rain, the Sun comes out from behind the clouds. If it is not too high in the sky, a rainbow appears, a half-circle of multi-coloured light.

The Sun's light looks yellowy-white to us, but in fact it is made up of a number of different colours. When sunlight passes through a drop of water, the rays of light are bent slightly. Each of the different colours of the light is bent at a slightly different angle.

This is how a drop of water can break up a sunbeam and make us see lots of different colours. After a storm, the millions of drops of water hanging in the sky break up the white light into a rainbow. The red colour is always at the outside of the curve, then come orange, yellow, green, blue, indigo and finally violet at the inside.
You can make your own rainbow by sprinkling a fine jet of water between yourself and the Sun.

You have the best view of a rainbow when the Sun is behind you. Usually rainbows are best early in the morning or in the evening when the Sun is low in the sky.

Sometimes when the water drops are large enough, the Sun's rays are reflected twice inside each drop. Two rainbows are formed, one inside another, and their colours are opposite ways round.

Snow is water transformed into ice crystals.

Stars in the snow

If the air gets very cold very quickly, falling to below 0 degrees Celsius, the clouds lose heat and the drops of water inside them turn to tiny needles of ice. As these fall through the sky, the ice needles stick together and make starry snow crystals.

These crystals cling together in a geometric way: they always have six branches, making six-rayed snow stars. If crystals fall in a wind, then they collide with each other forming flakes.

A snowflake is made of a few ice needles with a lot of air among them. This is rather like a duvet made of feathers; there is lots of air trapped in with the feathers. Freshly fallen snow is very light, but later it packs down into hard ice.

Snow that doesn't melt each summer grows into a glacier.

When you make a snowman, you need to press the snow into shape. This pushes out the air from between the ice needles so that the snow holds together.
If it freezes the next night, the snowman begins to turn into ice. He will last a long time then, even after the rest of the snow melts. It's much the same when snow in the mountains turns into glacier ice.

In the mountains, up above 3,000 metres, it is cold all the year round. It never rains. Here, when the clouds drop moisture, it always falls as snow. In the intense cold, the snow doesn't melt, even in summer. Year after year the snow grows thicker, freezing and thawing a little each day and night. The snow becomes old and mature and turns into ice.

A glacier is an enormous river of ice.
It flows slowly, slowly downhill from the mountain tops towards the valley, travelling over the rocky surface. The ice cracks where it goes over a steep slope or round bends in the valley. As it is solid it cannot flow easily and quickly round corners. These cracks which open in the glacier are the crevasses so dangerous for mountain climbers; they are sometimes as much as 60 metres deep.

Crevasses open and close again as the glacier moves. When the glacier travels down a steep slope on the mountain, it makes an ice-fall. This is like a waterfall which is formed when an ordinary river goes over a steep slope.
The ice-fall is made of jumbled blocks of broken glacier ice, called seracs. The ice in the seracs is blue when the ice is dense and hard, and white when it still contains air bubbles.

How is a weather forecast made?

By looking at the clouds and the wind, we can tell what kind of weather is on its way. Meteorologists use all kinds of instruments designed to tell what is happening in the atmosphere.

People who live by the weather, like farmers and fishermen, understand nature's clues about the sunshine, rain and storms. They look out for swallows flying low and crows gathering together, as well as for seagulls flying close to houses.

<u>A meteorologist's work</u>

These days information about the weather comes from all around the world at all hours of the day and night. First, a computer processes the data. Then meteorologists, people who study the weather, draw up maps of the world's weather patterns. By reading the maps, they can tell what the weather is going to do over the next day or so.

Where does this information come from? Weather stations on the ground have barometers to measure the atmospheric pressure, the weight of the air. When bad weather is coming, the pressure drops; we say the barometer is falling. A weather-vane shows the direction of the wind. An anemometer shows its speed. Weather stations also contain a thermometer which records the highest and lowest temperatures.

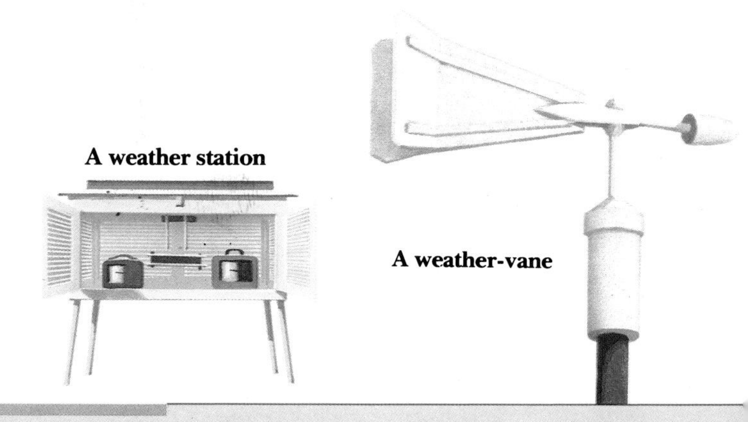

Using satellites and radar for weather forecasting

A hygrometer records how damp the air is. The stations also have a pluviometer to collect and measure how much rain has fallen.

Measuring the weather from air balloons

Special weather balloons are filled with hydrogen and carry instruments high into the atmosphere. The very light hydrogen gas floats the balloons up to 20 or 30 kilometres above the Earth. The balloons carry with them a radio transmitter and a radar reflector.
The transmitter continually sends information down to the ground about temperature, atmospheric pressure and the dampness of the air. Radar trackers on the ground follow the drifting balloon.
At sea, four thousand weather ships also help collect information about the world's weather.

A weather balloon with measuring equipment

Satellites watch the weather too.

They take photos and measure the Earth's weather. This is all added to the data bank at the weather centre.

Anemometer

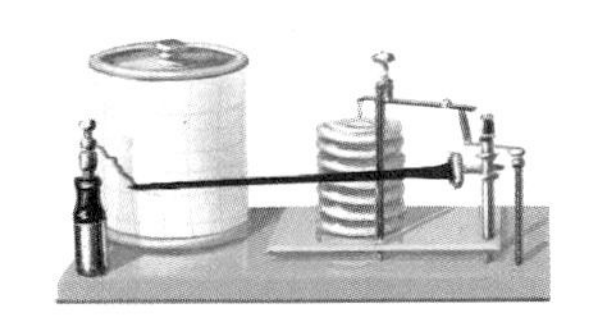

Barometer

A satellite

Why do we need weather forecasts?

We all want to know what the weather will do. Fishermen need to know how rough the sea will be, farmers need to know if there will be a frost, aircraft pilots want to choose their routes to use favourable winds, and people on holiday want to know if it's going to be sunny.

Our blue planet

Photos taken from satellites show that the Earth is about three-quarters covered in water. Almost half is covered by the Pacific Ocean, and the other oceans and seas make up the rest. Under the water there are volcanoes, mountains and deep, steep-sided valleys.

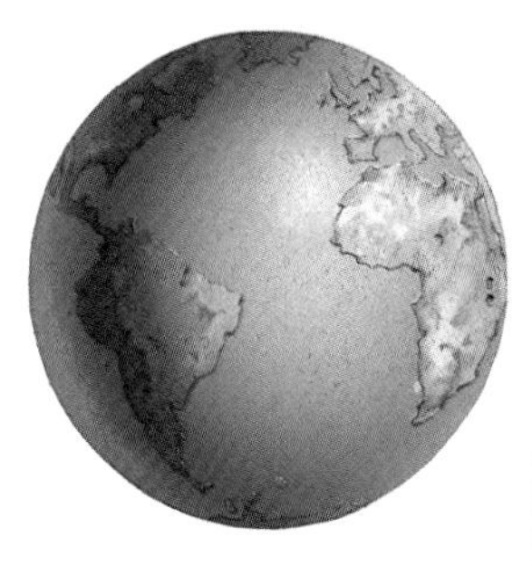

Atlantic Ocean

Pacific Ocean

The Pacific Ocean is the largest of all oceans. On its own it is bigger than all the continents put together.

The Indian Ocean is small, and lies between India and Africa. **The Arctic Ocean** is furthest north and surrounds the North Pole.

The Atlantic is shaped like a great letter S between Europe and Africa, and the two Americas. It is the youngest ocean, formed over the last two hundred million years, as the Americas gradually moved further and further away from Europe and Africa. When you look at a map, you can see how these great continents once fitted together – their coastlines still match, like parts of a jig-saw puzzle.

The mysterious depths of the ocean

The ocean floors are far from being flat boring plains. The Earth's longest mountain chain runs under the oceans, hidden from us by the deep water. Even before it was possible to explore the submarine depths, we knew that these mountains were made of volcanic rock. It is these active volcanoes which are pushing apart the continents.

Fifty million years separate each of these globes. The third one shows the Earth as it is now. Each year the Americas move 2 centimetres further from Europe and Africa.

The kingdom of the deep is another world.

For the last half century the oceans have been explored by scientists in submarines. They have begun to unlock the secrets of the deep.

The abyss, where the ocean is more than 2,000 metres deep, covers over half the surface of our planet. Only 1,700 metres down it is totally dark. **No light penetrates to this depth. It is also very cold in the ocean deeps.** The temperature is only 2 or 3 degrees Celsius at 2,000 metres down. Brrr! In some places it even reaches zero, but the water doesn't freeze because it's so salty. No seaweed grows in the deep, dark ocean and the creatures that live there are quite unlike anything else on the Earth. Many species which disappeared from the surface millions of years ago still survive in the abyss. The fish are often blind, with a huge upturned mouth, and a very soft body.

50 metres down, divers from a mini-submarine are filming a seaweed-covered wreck.

The ocean waters are always moving.

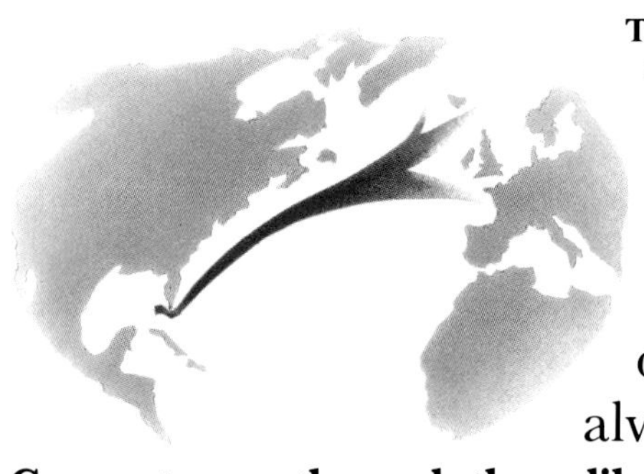

The Gulf Stream comes north-westwards from the Gulf of Mexico.

The waters of the seas and of the great oceans are always moving.

Currents run through them like rivers.
They are created when warm water meets cold water, and by the spinning of the Earth.

The currents also begin where water which is more salty meets up with less salty water. The most famous ocean current is the Gulf Stream. Fishermen discovered it long ago, when they were tracking schools of whales. The whales follow the warm water of the Gulf Stream, but they never swim in it. The Gulf Stream brings warm water and a warm climate to European shores. Ships use it to help them along on their voyage towards Europe, but when they travel back to America, they go south to avoid it, as it would slow them down.

In 1947, Thor Heyerdahl, a Norwegian, used the Humboldt current to float a grass raft, the Kon-Tiki, from South America to the Polynesian Islands in the Pacific Ocean. It took three months.

At the seashore, the sea level rises and falls regularly. This is what we call the tides.
The Moon and the Sun's gravity pull the Earth's water towards them. This makes the sea-level rise and fall as the Earth spins. Out in the Oceans, the change in water level is tiny. At the shore, though, you can see it clearly. The sea-level rises for six hours then, just as slowly, falls again. There are two of these tides every day and each rise and fall together takes twelve hours; the high tide is about 50 minutes later each day.

Sea-birds resting on the surface of the sea bob up and down on the waves. The waves rise and fall, but do not move forward.

When the wind blows, it makes waves on the surface of the sea.
Wind causes ripples on the surface of the water, which grow to become ocean waves. At the seashore, the waves break against the land, in a mass of white spray. Out at sea, a big storm can raise waves taller than a house. Ships are built to be able to sail through such storm waves.

Sometimes you see waves on the sea even when there is no wind. Waves are born a long way from where they finally come ashore. It's just the same as the ripples which travel outwards when you drop a pebble into a pool of water. Waves raised by winds off the coast of America come lapping at the shores of Europe, 5,000 kilometres away.

Only the surface of the sea is disturbed by the waves. Down below, the fish swim quietly in calm waters. Sometimes, though, undersea earthquakes create waves deep down which ships on the surface know nothing about.

Tidal waves can be huge, dangerous mountains of water.
They may be whipped up by violent storms during which atmospheric pressure is low. This causes the ocean water to lift above its normal level. These are tidal surges. True tidal waves are caused when there is an earthquake under the sea, or when volcanoes erupt and push aside the sea water. These waves rush over whole islands, crushing trees and houses on their way.

Pack ice from frozen seawater, icebergs from frozen land

Most of the Earth's fresh water is frozen into ice at the North and South Poles.

Water which is frozen from the sea is called pack ice. It builds up in freezing winter cold around the seashores near the North and South Poles. In summer, waves break up the pack ice, so it floats away, and eventually melts. The ocean at the North Pole is permanently covered with thick pack ice which never melts completely.

Iceberg from the North Pole

Icebergs are like frozen castles floating on the sea. Where do they come from?

Icebergs are made of fresh water. They began life as huge glaciers covering the land in polar areas. Antarctica, Greenland and the mountains of Alaska are where many are born. When the glaciers reach the sea, they float out over the heavy salty water, and eventually break up. The icy fragments, some of which are huge, are called icebergs. The word actually means ice mountain, and that is what they look like.

A South Pole iceberg

North Pole icebergs are usually crazy, pointed shapes; those from the South Pole are more often flat.

Icebergs float around the Polar seas and are dangerous to ships passing nearby. Only a small part of the iceberg shows above the sea: more than six times as much of the iceberg is hidden under water.

Most of an iceberg is hidden under water.

Nowadays, there is an international patrol which surveys the danger zones so ships can be warned off.

The coasts are battlegrounds between the sea and the land.

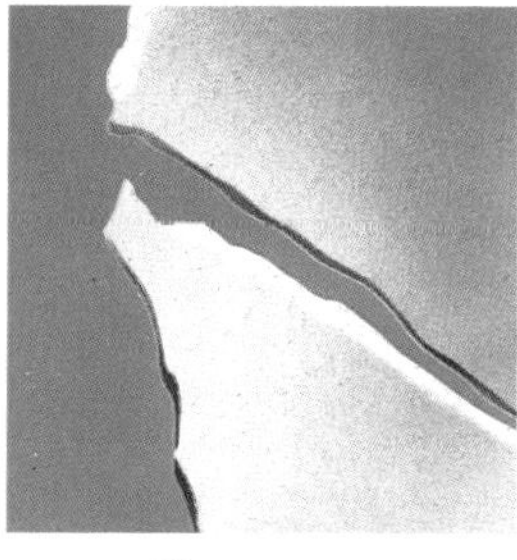

Estuary

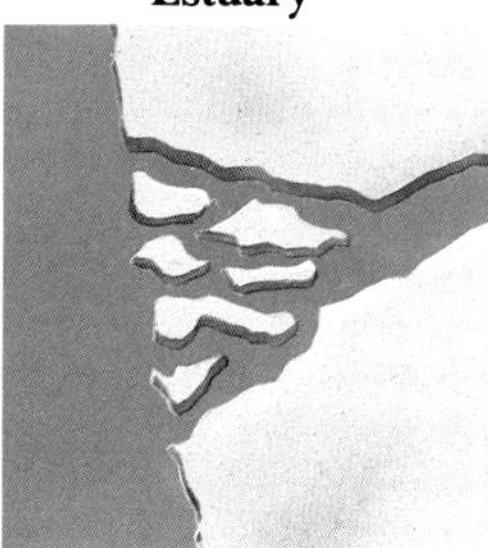

Delta

Along the length of the coastline, the scenery changes every few kilometres. Some coasts have rugged cliffs plunging down to the sea. Elsewhere a sandy bay is followed by cliffs, and round the next corner there may be an inlet with a beach. There are also places where flat, sandy or pebble beaches stretch as far as the eye can see. In the tropics you may even find offshore islands or coral reefs with lagoons.

Where the river meets the sea

From its inland source the river flows towards the sea. At its mouth the fresh water pours into the salty ocean.
A river may end in an estuary, a wide mouth. Here the up and down movement of the sea tides is noticeable inland, far up the river.
Sometimes the river carries sand which it drops as it nears the sea. Sandbanks are formed through which the river wanders making new paths for itself. This is a delta. A lagoon is a stretch of calm water protected behind a barrier of land.

Lagoon

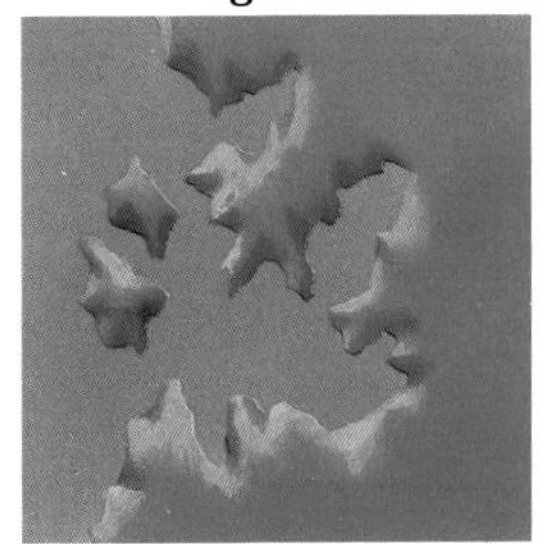

Fiord

The fiords of Norway are deep valleys carved out by glaciers in the Ice Age. Now the glaciers have melted, and the valleys are flooded by the sea.

The coast is always changing.

It may be eroded by the wind and the sea or new land may be built up by sand and gravel carried by rivers.

Mountains are the rooftops of the Earth.

There are mountains on every continent. Their lofty peaks, deep, dark valleys and barren rocks used to make people afraid. They believed that gods or demons lived on the summits. Some mountains are so hard to climb that they might as well be the stairway to the sky... or to heaven. Today many mountain summits have been climbed by brave people, although many have died trying.

What is inside the Earth?

Like an apple, the Earth has a core. It also has flesh – the mantle, and a skin – called the crust. We could never take a journey to the centre of the Earth as it is far too hot, and the pressure would squash us almost to nothing. We live on the thin crust of cool, more or less solid rock which covers the Earth.

Millions of years ago, all the continents were joined together as a single, huge land mass. Over time they have drifted apart. Some are still moving apart, while others are moving towards each other.

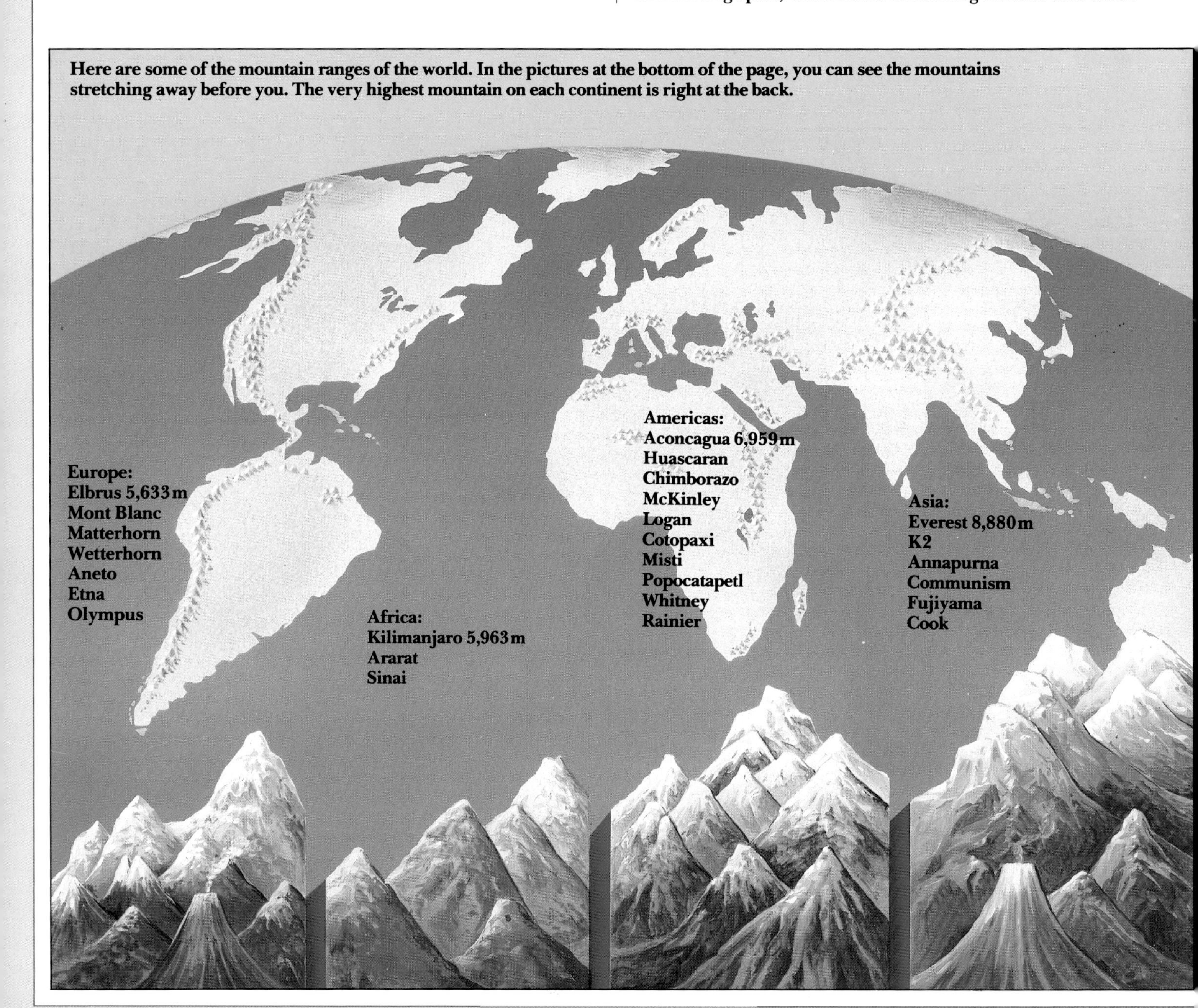

The Earth's mighty internal energy folds and shatters rocks.

How are mountains formed?

Powerful currents within the mantle push up on the Earth's crust.

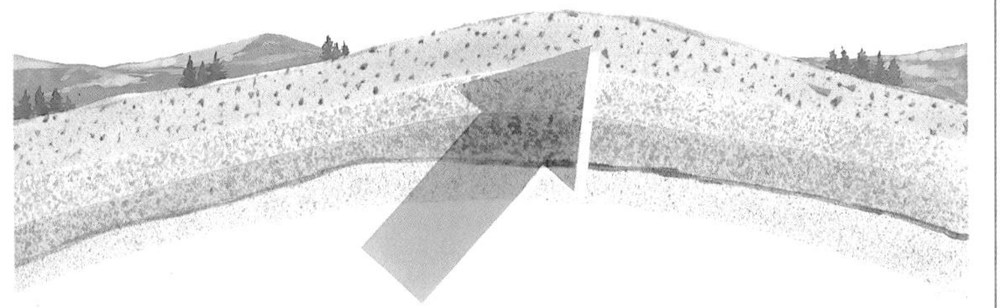

Pushed by the pressure from below, the rocks of the Earth's crust fold, crack, or lift up.

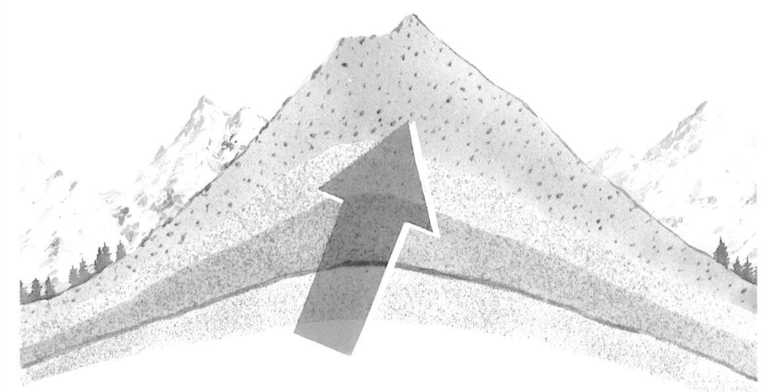

Some mountains are growing higher by as much as a metre every thousand years.

The Earth's outer skin, the crust, is not whole. It is made of many different pieces which fit together like bits of a huge jig-saw puzzle. Inside the Earth, the mantle is moving. So strong are these mantle movements, that the jig-saw pieces of crust get pushed around over the surface of the Earth. Even plates as large as the continents are moving, though very, very slowly.

When two plates push against each other, the rocks at the touching edges fold up and crack. The Himalaya mountains are the result of India moving northwards towards Asia. This collision has been taking place over millions of years.

Young mountains are being eroded just as fast as they are growing.

The Himalayas and the European Alps are young mountains. They have only been growing for the last 40 million years! They are still growing now, but the wind, snow, glaciers and rain are already wearing them away, carrying rocks and stones from the summits into the deep valleys. Cornwall, and the mountains of Wales and Scotland are old mountains. They stopped growing long ago and their slopes have become rounded off over the course of hundreds of millions of years.

Formation of the Himalayas

Mountains form huge chains which reach across continents.

The Sherpa people who live in the mountains of Nepal are very strong. They can carry loads as heavy as themselves.

Very few mountains stand all on their own. Usually there are long chains of mountains, one overlapping with the next. There are two main mountain chains on the Earth. The first includes the Alps, the mountains of Greece, Iran, and the Himalayas. The other chain encircles the Pacific Ocean: it includes the Rocky Mountains of North America, the Andes in the south, the New Zealand Alps, and the mountains of Japan.

The mountain peaks are barriers which slow down the clouds.

To get over the mountains, the clouds must rise higher into the sky. Up there the air is colder and cannot hold so much water, so it begins to rain or snow. It's always raining or snowing on the sides of the mountains which face towards the clouds as they arrive, while the far sides are quite dry. Snow and glacier ice provide reserves of fresh water for streams.

The Himalayas and the Andes are mountain fortresses.

On Lake Titicaca, nearly 4,000 metres up in the mountains, the Indians of South America use bundles of reeds to make canoes.

Mountain scenery changes with altitude and with the amount of sunshine on the slopes.
The further up you climb in the mountains, the colder it gets. The trees are smaller higher up, and gradually they give way to shrubs, then to the grass of the alpine meadows.
Higher still only mosses and lichens can stand the cold. Eventually you arrive at the land of eternal snow.
Here glaciers are born.

In spite of the intense cold, people live even in the highest mountain valleys.
In the Himalayan valleys, on the south side which gets all the rain from the summer monsoon, people have sculpted the slopes into terraces to cultivate as much of the land as possible.
The higher mountain plateaux and slopes are used as pasture for rearing and grazing ponies, sheep and yaks.

The Andes mountains are called Cordillera – a word meaning rope in Spanish.
They stretch 7,500 kilometres from Mexico in the north to Tierra del Fuego at the very southern tip of South America.

Everest is the highest mountain in the Himalayas, at 8,000 metres high. It forms the border between Nepal and Tibet. On the lower slopes of the mountain, terraces are made for growing rice.

The Indians of Bolivia and Peru are able to live and to herd their llamas even as high up as 4,500 metres.

The high mountains, called sierras, surround a vast high plain, the altiplano, at 3,000 to 4,000 metres up. Here the air is thin, the winds are strong, few animals can survive and even the plants find life difficult.

Machu Picchu in Peru, built by the ancient Incas as a fortress city about 500 years ago, was only rediscovered in 1911.

Volcanoes: mountains which breathe fire

Volcanoes shudder and throb with escaping hot gases, ash and molten rock. Where does it all come from? It comes from inside the Earth, from parts of the mantle where rocks are melting. Sometimes the molten rocks escape through cracks in the crust. This is what makes a volcanic eruption.

Inside a volcano: 1. Reservoir of magma 2. Chimney 3. Cone with crater at the top

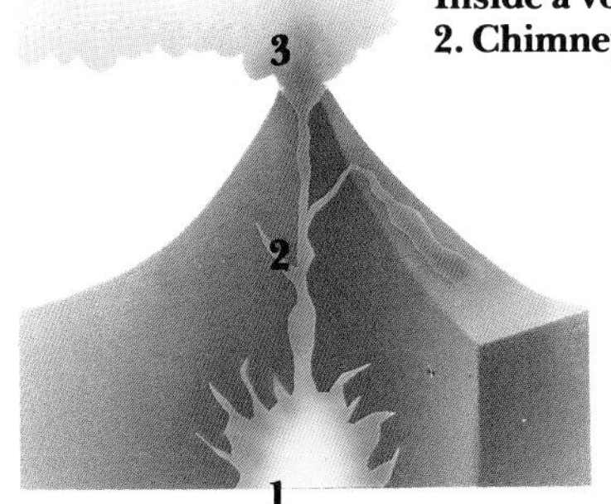

Inside the Earth it is very hot, perhaps as much as 5,000 degrees Celsius. So some of the rock inside the Earth melts, making little pockets of molten rock called magma. The magma forces its way up through cracks here and there in the Earth's surface. It spurts out into the air, pushed up by the pressure and hot gases inside the Earth. A volcano is erupting!

Lava is red when it is hot. As it cools, it turns grey or black.

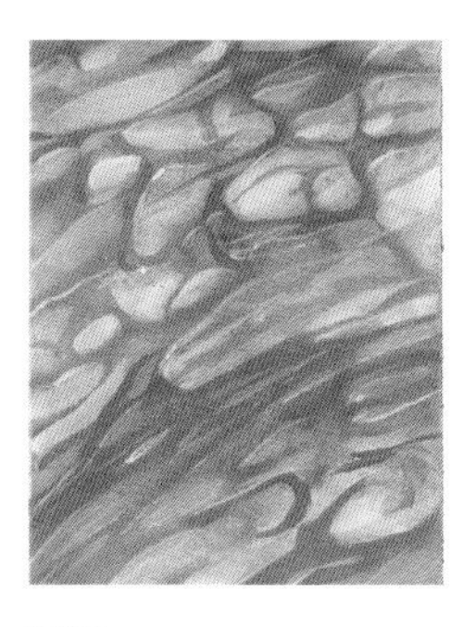

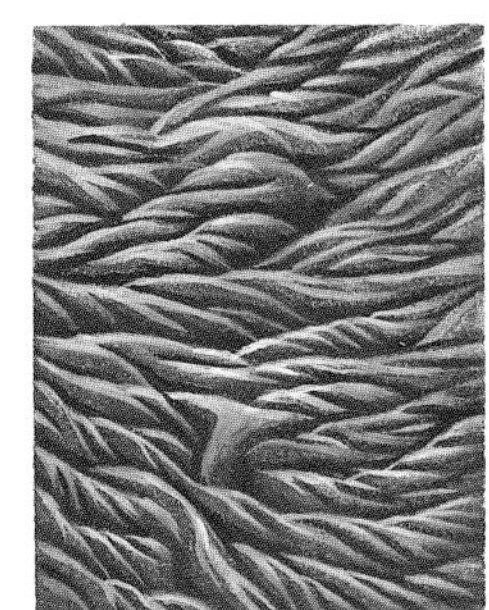

When magma escapes from the Earth, we call it lava.

If lava is very thick and sticky, it solidifies at the crater, or is hurled up into the air as big boulders, ash and fine dust. If the lava is very liquid and runny, it flows like a river down the sides of the cone, or makes a red hot lake in the crater.

Volcanoes are born, they live their lives and eventually die.

1. During 1943, at Paricutin in Mexico, a farmer was working in his field when suddenly the ground started to shake.

It is rare that somebody sees a volcano when it first appears. Only a few volcanoes are born each century.

2. The next day, there was a volcano where the field had been.

In 1963, Surtsey, a new volcano, burst out of the sea off the coast of Iceland. An island had been born. Surtsey erupted for four years, with hot lava and ash falling into the foaming sea. It is hard to predict where the next new volcano will be. It, too, may be an island in the sea.

3. The lava flooded over the nearby village. Only the church tower could be seen above the lava.

A volcano is said to be extinct, or dead, when it hasn't erupted for tens of thousands of years. Sometimes, though, a volcano which seems extinct may simply be dormant, or asleep. One day it may wake up and erupt again. Between eruptions, wind, snow and rain wear away the cone. How much is worn away shows how long it is since the volcano last erupted.

The longer a volcano has been dormant, the more spectacular is its reawakening! In 1980, a huge explosion blew off the top of Mount St Helens, in the western United States. This one explosion reduced the height of the volcano by 430 metres.

Cotopaxi, almost on the Equator, in Ecuador, is dormant at the moment.

A dormant volcano may be cool enough for water to form a lake in the crater. Sometimes the water in these lakes is warm or even hot.

Some old volcanoes have huge craters many kilometres across.

Especially big craters form when the top of the mountain collapses as the magma empties out of it. Sometimes the force of the eruption literally blows the top off the mountain. These very big collapsed craters are known as calderas.

In search of the secrets of the volcanoes

There are more volcanoes in the sea than there are on land.

Nearly all of the sea bed is made up of lava formed in the last 200 million years. These are amongst the youngest rocks on Earth. Cooled quickly by the sea water, the lava sometimes hardens into strange pillowy shapes. Deep in the ocean, volcanic gases escape from cracks in the sea bed. These are rich in metals like zinc and lead. The metals come out in billowing clouds of gas which are called black smokers.

Can people fight against the huge power of a volcano?

If a volcano is about to erupt, people and animals can only get out of the way. When a volcano in southern Iceland awoke after a 5,000 years sleep, people were able to escape danger, though their homes were buried under ash and lava. To stop the lava-flow which was threatening to block the town harbour, the Icelanders doused it with water from high pressure hoses. This hardened the lava, and stopped it in its tracks.

If we are to stop people being killed by volcanoes, it is important to learn when the volcanoes are likely to erupt. This is the task of volcanologists.

Volcanologists are like doctors and volcanoes are their patients.

They listen to volcanoes to find out what is happening and judge when the next eruption will happen. As a doctor uses a stethoscope and a thermometer, volcanologists use instruments to listen to the movement of magma inside the volcano. They measure any swelling of the slopes of the volcano cone, and the temperature of the volcano's gases to discover if the volcano is going to become active.

Hardened lava from earlier eruptions can be bulldozed to make a wall to divert lava-flows.

Clouds of gas, rich in metals, pour from under-sea cracks.

There are more than 10,000 active volcanoes on the Earth.

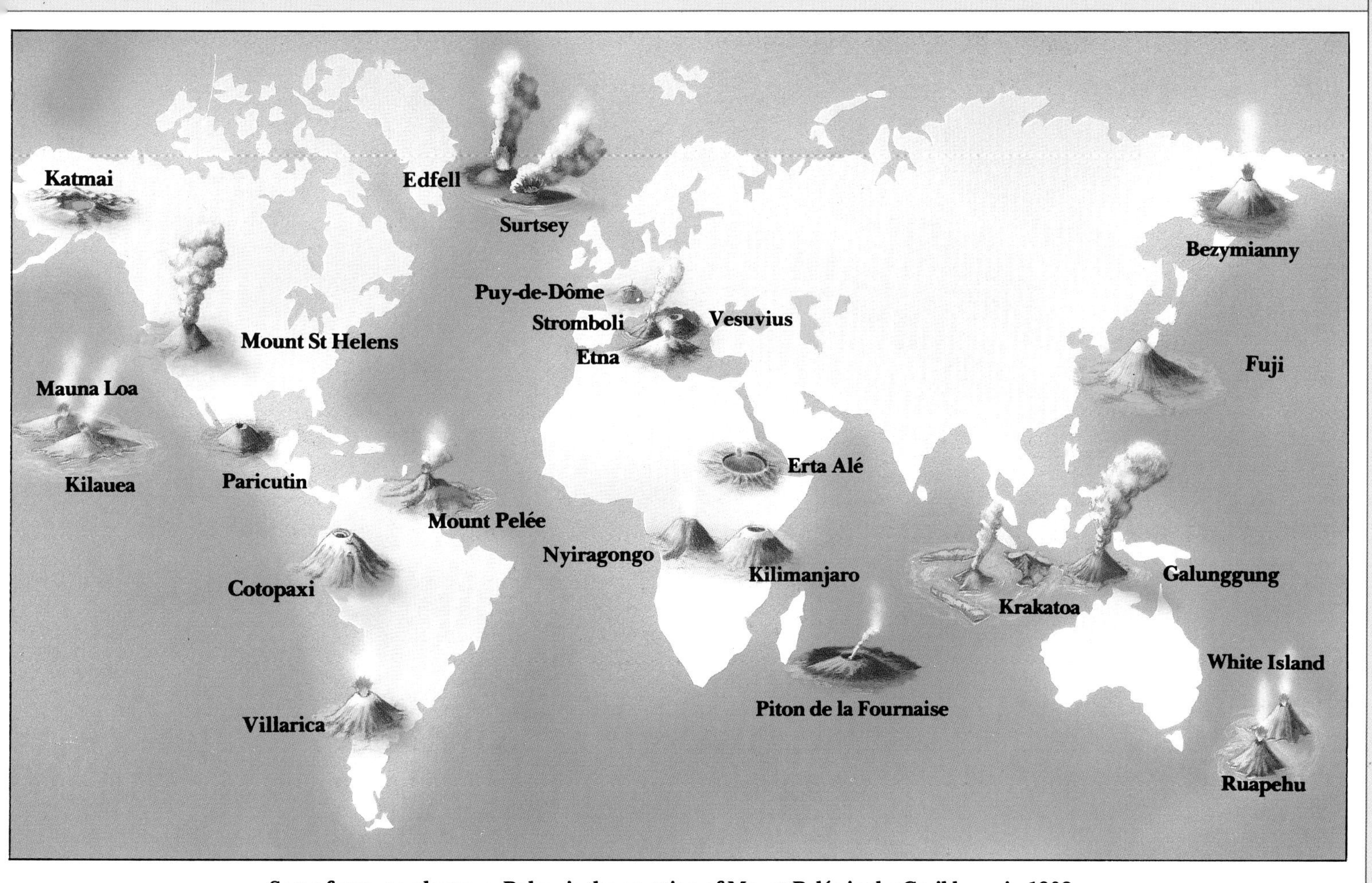

Some famous volcanoes. Below is the eruption of Mount Pelée in the Caribbean, in 1902.

What happens when the Earth's crust is broken?

Earthquakes only happen in certain parts of the world, called seismic zones. These are where the plates of crust which cover the Earth's surface meet each other. Inside the Earth, the mantle is always moving and this in turn moves the plates. When the tension gets too great, the rocks on the edges of the plates grate and grind against each other and the Earth's surface may crack.

Every minute an earthquake happens somewhere on the Earth. Most are small and are not felt. A few each year kill people and destroy their homes.

As the plates grind against each other, the rocks break and shock waves travel outwards, making the ground tremble. If a large amount of rock breaks, the earthquake will be a big one.

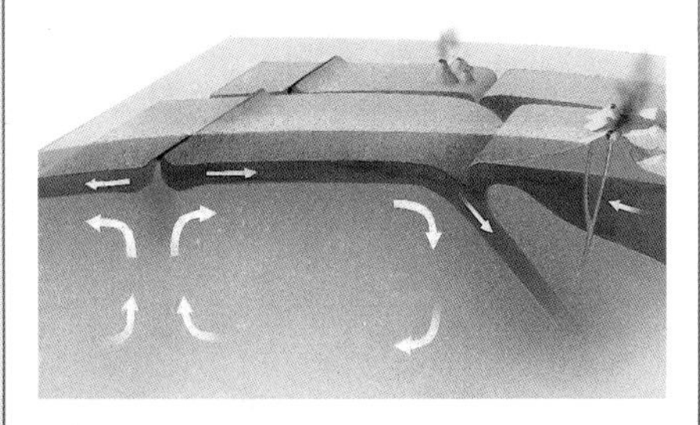

An earthquake

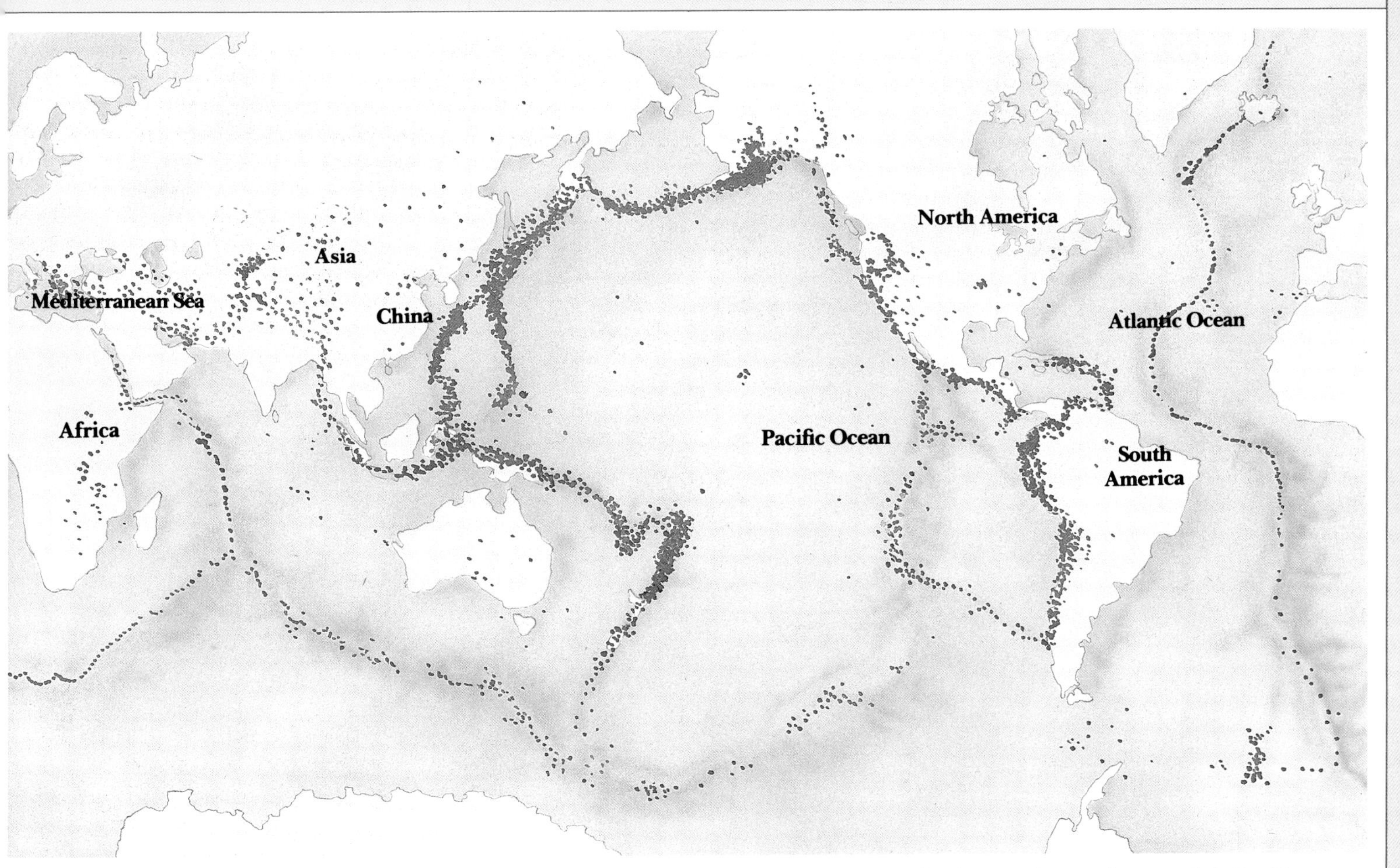

The most important seismic zones form a ring round the Pacific Ocean. A second zone runs from the Mediterranean to China. Others are in the mountain chains of the deep oceans.

Where do earthquakes begin?

Earthquakes start from a central focus, as far as 700 kilometres under the Earth's surface. Shock waves travel out in all directions as well as up to the ground. The place on the ground immediately above the focus is called the epicentre.

If you lived in a country where earthquakes were common, you'd know it's safest to get under a big piece of furniture as soon as you feel the shaking begin.

To record earthquakes, we use instruments called seismographs. These make a record of the size and shape of the shock waves travelling out from the earthquake through the rocks. From the trace the seismograph makes, we can grade earthquakes on the Richter scale, from 1 to 8. By looking at the damage and other effects, we measure, from 1 to 12, how intense an earthquake was at any place. In 1906, a quake of 8.3 on the Richter scale devastated the city of San Francisco. It caused damage at intensity 11.

A hidden world under the ground

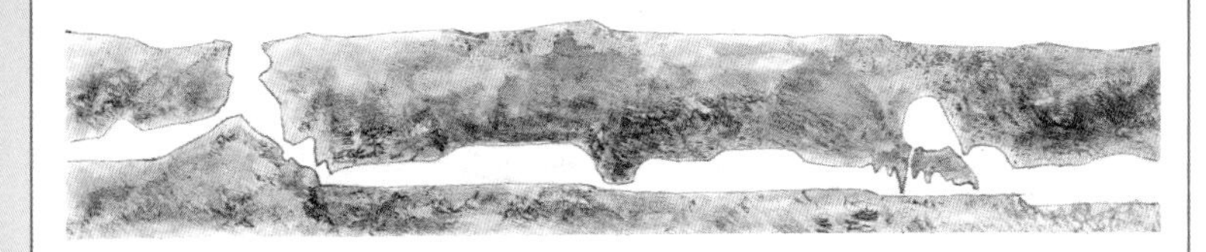

In limestone country, spectacular caves are formed underground. Some are enormous, even larger than the biggest cathedrals and office blocks. Rivers flow through these underground caverns, cascading in sparkling waterfalls to form pools and vast lakes. There's a whole world beneath our feet.

How are underground caves and rivers formed?

When it rains, much of the water seeps into the ground. In an area of limestone, the rainwater eats away the rock over millions of years. The limestone dissolves along the paths made by the water and slowly caves are formed.

The water eventually reaches a place where there's no more limestone, or it cannot travel downwards. This might be because the rocks are already full of water. The water is forced sideways and becomes an underground river, flowing downhill, just like a river above ground.

Eventually the water comes out into the light of day as a clear, clean spring, perhaps at the bottom of a deep valley.

Strange shapes grow in the caves.

Water drips off the roof and splashes on to the floor below. Very, very slowly, over thousands of years, the minerals from the water form into stone icicles. These hang from the roof or grow up from the floor where the drips fall. In time, the stalactites growing downwards meet the stalagmites rising from the floor of the cave.

Speleologists explore underground caves.

The caves look like fairyland with organ pipes, melting candles, tree trunks and draped curtains. The great columns which seem to hold up the roofs of the caves are perhaps the most amazing to visitors. And all this came just from dripping water!

Speleologists study a whole underground world – the caves themselves (geology), the underground rivers (hydrogeology), the animals and plants in the caves (zoology and botany). Speleologists, for their own safety, need also to know how humans react to cold and damp in caves, as they spend a lot of time in them.

Exploring underground

To be a speleologist you need to overcome many dangers. Cavers carry sophisticated equipment to help them through these dangers: ropes, rope ladders, lights, radios to stay in contact with each other and with the support team above ground, and inflatable rubber boats, maybe with motors, for following underground rivers.

Strong workers: water, wind and frost

Rock towers in Canada

If you build a sandcastle on the beach, it gets washed away by the waves. If you dam a river with some pebbles to make a little pool, these too will be swept away by the river one day, after it has rained heavily. The surface of the Earth is continually being swept, reshaped and eroded by rain, ice, wind and rivers.

When cliffs are worn away by the waves, parts of them collapse. The loose rocks become pebbles, which the waves toss about, wearing the cliffs away more . . . .

Along the coast, waves beat against the shore.
The power of waves is enormous. It lifts pebbles and boulders, and hurls them against the cliffs. In time, this wears away even the hardest rock.
Wherever the rock is softer, it is worn away faster, forming caves, bays and inlets. Harder rock takes longer to erode, forming steep rugged headlands, standing out against the battering of the waves.

Rainstorms reshape the land.
In a storm, rainwater percolates in through the soil or runs away over the rocks. In the mountains it pours as torrents over the rocky ground. Wherever it goes, it carries some rock, mud or sand grains with it.
A very heavy flood can move a whole mountainside. Landslides carry away these broken fragments of rock as pebbles and boulders.

Underground water in Borneo has worn away a great mountain of limestone: all that is left are these strange pinnacles above the forest.

In the mountains it is ice which wears away the rocks.
Snow and rainwater seep into cracks in the rock, and turn to ice in the cold, mountain weather. As water freezes, it expands, with a force strong enough to break rocks apart. Little by little, over millions of years, mountains are worn away to become hills, and in the end they are almost worn down altogether, leaving a plain.

In the deserts, where there is no water, wind wears away the rocks.
The wind lifts grains of sand. Even in a breeze, the wind acts like a sand-blaster on the rocks, eroding them. The sand dunes which are formed may be long ridges running parallel to the direction of the wind, or crescent-shaped, their points facing into the wind.

These old volcanoes have been extinct for a long time. Their summits have been rounded off by the rain, and their slopes made more gentle.

What happens to all the rock that is worn away?
It is carried down to the valleys and plains and eventually fills up even the deepest and largest valleys.
At the foot of every mountain stream, there is a fan of broken rock; along valley glaciers, there is a moraine of rocky fragments; at the foot of a cliff, there is sand or pebbles. In the desert, there are sand dunes.
In time these rock fragments will make new rocks.

So everywhere, all over the Earth's surface, rock is being worn away and new rock is being made. The surface of the Earth is truly in perpetual motion, always renewing itself, always recycling itself.

Rainwater even wears away granite, the hardest of rocks. It seeps in between the tiny grains of the rock, and prises them apart.

A map of the Earth today

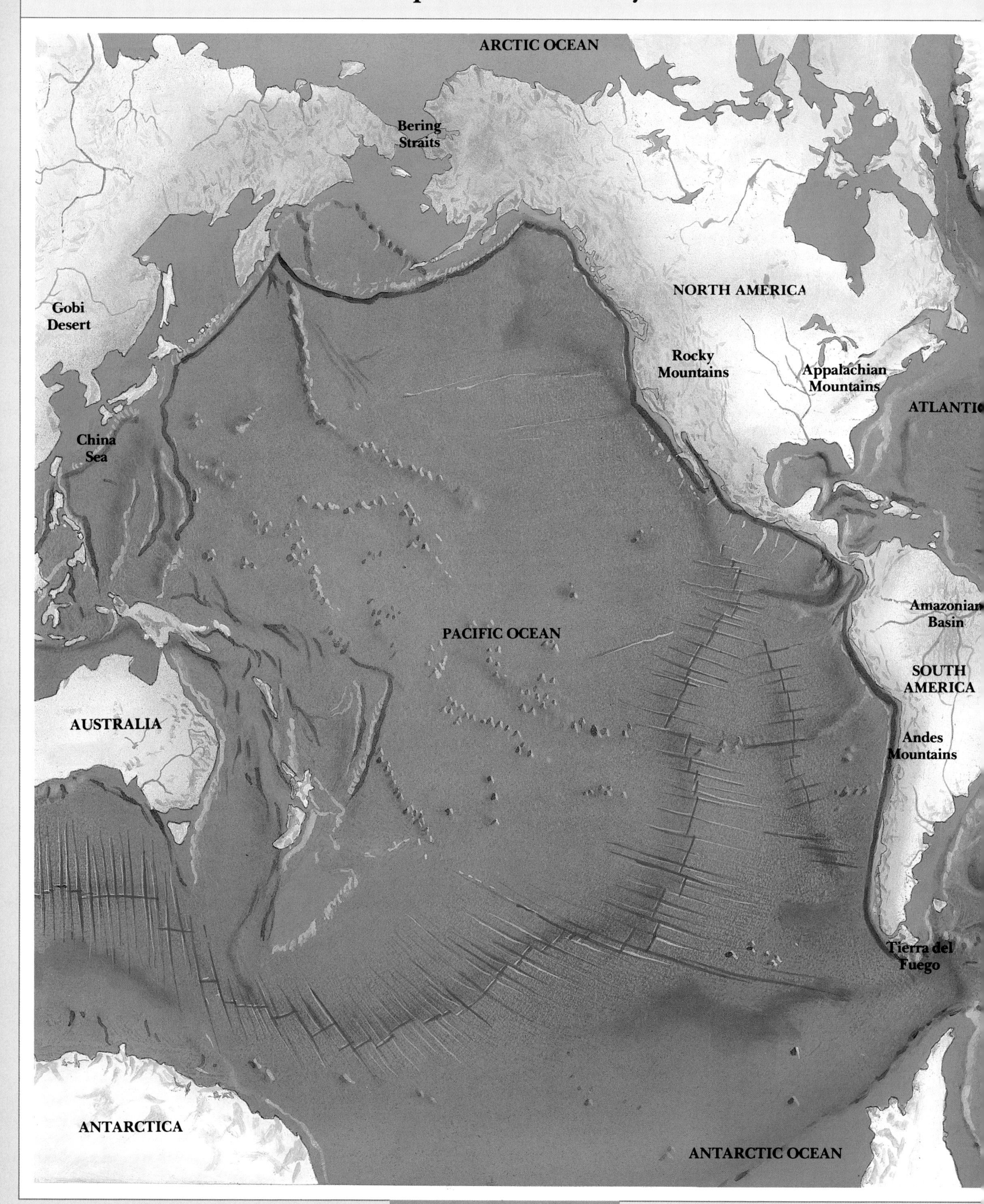

The Earth will never stop changing.

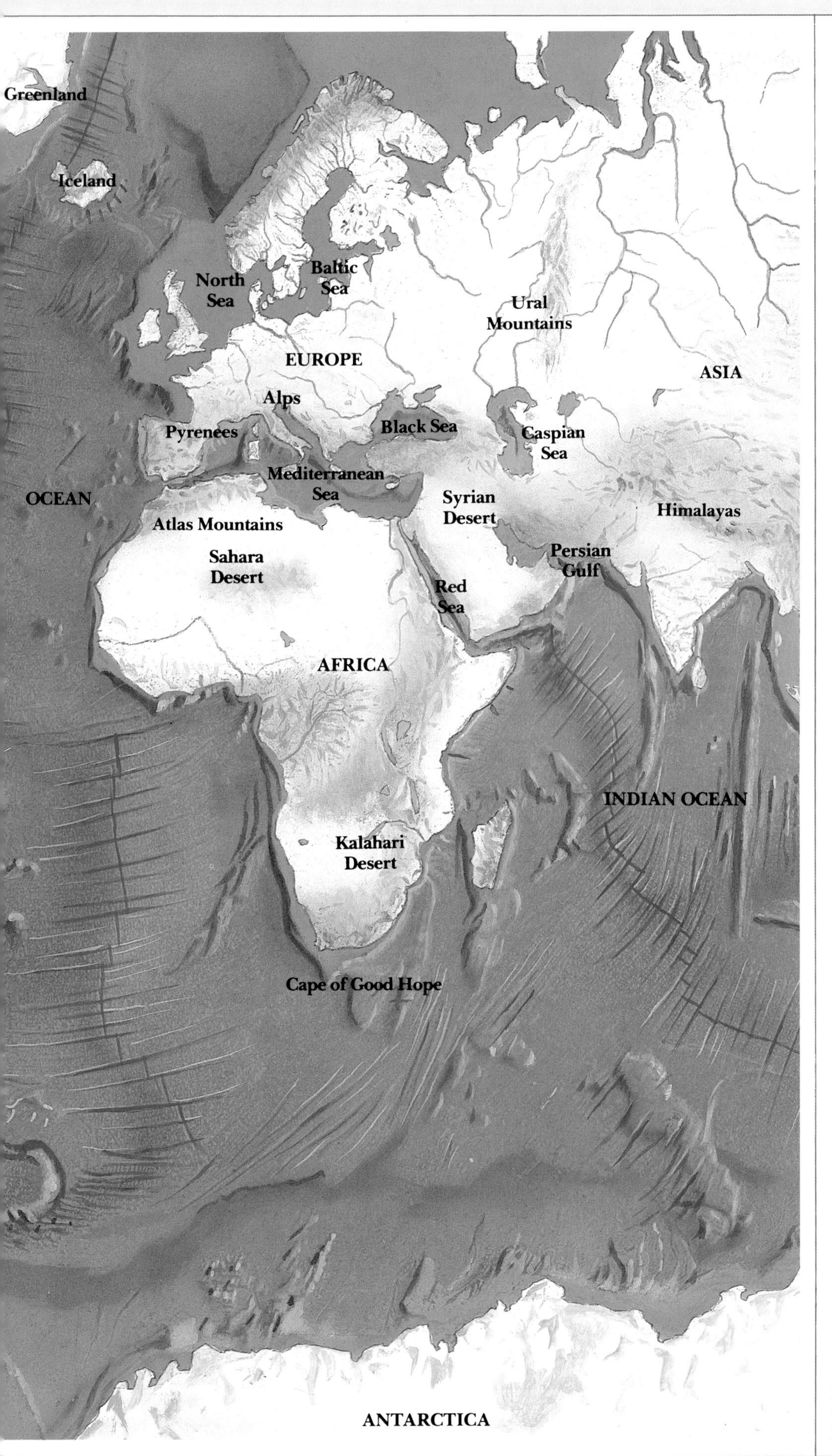

The Earth is a living planet. It is always changing, but so very slowly that we do not realise what is happening.
Earthquakes and volcanic eruptions remind us in a brutal way that the Earth is alive. But we also know, even without seeing it, that mountains are growing, and that at the same time they are being worn away.
And new rocks are being laid down, like thick blankets, filling valleys and plains.
Even whole continents are moving, some getting closer together, others moving apart.
Climates are changing. Less than a million years ago, Europe and North America were covered with glaciers.
There have been humans on the Earth for only a few hundred thousand years; this period is just a brief instant in the whole history of the Earth.

Imagine that the Earth was formed ten days ago: man has existed for less than one second!

Games and activities, intriguing facts, a quiz, records, sayings, useful addresses and places to visit, a glossary, followed by the index

■ Did you know?

The distance from the Earth to the Sun is 148 million kilometres.

The diameter of the Sun is 110 times greater than the diameter of the Earth. The Sun's volume is 1,300,000 times greater than the Earth's.

How can you tell from the Moon's shape whether it's on the way to being full Moon or new Moon? When the shape makes a 'd', the old Moon is dying. It is always the lit part which faces towards the Sun.

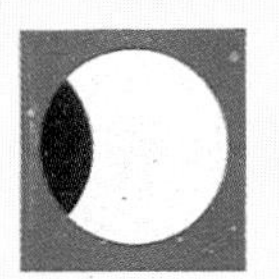

Winter in the northern hemisphere is the shortest season: it lasts 89 days. Summer lasts 93 days. So of course in the southern hemisphere, it is winter which is the longest season, with 93 days.

Not only are mountains high, they are heavy as well. Their bulk adds so much extra weight to the Earth's crust that the whole thickness of the plate sinks down a little, into the soft mantle below.
The mountains would be even higher if they did not sink in.

Why does the Sun look red when it's rising and setting? Because there is always a layer of dust hanging above the surface of the ground. In the mornings and evenings the rays of the Sun reach us at an angle, travelling a long way through this dust. The dust scatters the blue light away, and only the red reaches us.

You can tell the time with a sundial. This could be small enough to go in your pocket, or it might be made of stone and built into the wall of your house.

People learned a long time ago how to tell the time of day from the Sun, using a stick planted in the ground. This is called a gnomon. For many hundreds of years the gnomon was the only way of telling the time. The sundial is just an improvement on the gnomon.

You could use your shadow to tell the time, but you'd need to stand still for a long time! You would know when it was midday, because that's the time when your shadow would be shortest – when the Sun is highest in the sky.

Mark out where your shadow falls at various times of day, and you can become a sundial!

The seas and the oceans cover about 75% of the Earth. Their average depth is 3,800 metres. If the Earth's surface could be levelled out completely, there would be water 750 metres deep everywhere!

Sea water begins to freeze when the temperature is lower than minus 2 degrees Celsius. Ice floats on the water when it's that cold, and it may be very thick. Even so, the submarine *Nautilus* found its way up through the pack ice and came to the surface exactly at the North Pole in 1954.

Thunderstorms: In 1752, Benjamin Franklin proved that lightning wasn't a great fire in the sky as some people had thought. He showed it is a spark of electricity. He flew a kite in a thunderstorm, with a metal key on the end of the kite string which he was holding in his hand.
He risked his life in doing this, but it helped him discover how to make lightning conductors to protect buildings in storms.

■ Legends about the Universe

Wonderful stories were made up long, long ago to explain how the Earth came to be. The people who made up these legends looked at things differently from the way we do now. The ancient Germans thought that Thor was the god of thunder. Whenever he was angry, he hit the sky with his hammer, making thunder and lightning.

Thousands of years ago, the creation of the Earth was described in stories about the lives of various gods.
The Greeks said that once upon a time there was nothing, and out of this came Gaia, the Earth and then Uranus, the sky. Their children were the Titans, the Cyclopes and the other giants. Cronos, their youngest son, wounded his father, so he himself could rule the Universe. To make sure nobody got rid of him, Cronos ate his own sons.

There are countless legends about the Sun:

The Sun god of the ancient Sumerians came out of a cave each morning and rode across the sky in a brilliant chariot of light. Each evening he drove the chariot back into the mountain.

For the ancient Egyptians the Sun god was Ra, who had a hawk's head on top of which was a sun disc. Another Sun god was the falcon-headed Horus, who took earthly shape in the pharaohs. The Egyptians also had different names for the Sun as it appeared at different times: Khepri was the rising Sun, Atum the setting Sun, Re the Sun at its height, and Aton the Sun's disc.

People were in awe of mountains because they believed that the gods lived there.
In many countries, people still travel long distances, through great dangers and intense cold to visit their gods in the mountains.

In Peru, millions of Indians go on a pilgrimage each spring into the Andes mountains. In the bitter cold they make their way to a sanctuary near the town of Cuzco. The Ukuku Indians take home with them some of the glacier ice, which they believe cures various illnesses.

Cronos's wife, Rhea, wanted to save her youngest son, Zeus from being killed by the ambitious Cronos. She tricked Cronos into swallowing a stone instead of eating Zeus, who grew up in hiding in a cave. Later, he forced his father to spit out all the children he'd eaten. Cronos and the Titans were sent to Tartarus, the underworld, and Zeus became supreme ruler of the world.

Zeus and his family were believed to live at the summit of Mount Olympus in Greece.
From there Zeus could throw thunderbolts at anyone who angered him. His wife, Hera, lived with him as well as various other gods and goddesses such as Demeter the goddess of the harvest; Apollo, god of music and prophecy and the most handsome of all the gods; Aphrodite, the goddess of love; and Artemis, the huntress. Poseidon, Zeus's brother, ruled over the sea.

■ Records – the first, the biggest, the longest

The greatest meteorite shower was in 1966 in Arizona, USA; nearly 2,300 meteorites passed overhead in just 20 minutes.

The Earth's nearest neighbour in space is the Moon. In 1609, Galileo was the first person to look at the Moon, through a simple telescope.

Man's first contact with the Moon was made in 1959 by a Russian space rocket, Luna II.

The greatest altitude on the Moon which man has so far reached is 7,830 metres in the Descartes Mountains. This was in 1972, and the climbers were the astronauts Young and Duke.

The longest eclipse of the Sun ever measured was 7 minutes and 8 seconds. This was in the Philippines in 1955.

You can fly along with the shadow of the eclipse, and so see it for longer. Concorde followed an eclipse of the Sun for 72 minutes in 1973.

In 1519 Magellan set sail on an expedition that circled the world for the first time. It took three years.
Out of the five ships which had set out to sail westwards right round the Earth, only one returned to Spain. This journey proved that the Earth was round. Later, in 1687, Newton showed that it is slightly flattened at the two poles.

Jupiter is the largest planet in the solar system: it is 1,323 times bigger than the Earth.

Mercury is the fastest at making its journey round the Sun.

The Earth's highest mountain is called Chomolungma, meaning goddess mother of the world in Tibetan. We know it as Everest after George Everest who first measured its height. In 1987, K2, another mountain in the Himalayan range, was remeasured as being a bit higher. K2 briefly became the highest mountain! The people who had climbed it suddenly became the people who had climbed the highest peak on the Earth. It was a mistake. Everest is really the highest mountain on the Earth. It's summit was first reached in 1953 by Sir Edmund Hillary of New Zealand and a Nepalese, Tenzing Norgay.

The highest mountain in Europe is an extinct volcano, Elbrus, 5,633 metres high, in the Caucasus mountains, in the USSR.

The highest mountain in the European Alps is Mont Blanc at 4,807 metres, on the border between France, Italy and Switzerland. It was first climbed in 1786. The road tunnel through the mountain is 11.6 kilometres long.

The biggest active volcano is Mauna Loa in Hawaii.
Since 1832, it has erupted every three and a half years.

The longest glacier is 402 metres long.
It is the Lambert Glacier in Antarctica.
In the Alps, the Mer de Glace and the Glacier du Géant put together would be 13 kilometres long.

The fastest moving glacier is the Quarayac in Greenland, which travels between 20 and 24 metres a day.

The biggest icebergs could be as much as 700 metres high, but only 70 metres of this would be above sea level.
Some are up to 2 kilometres across.
The biggest observed was 167 metres high.

The largest desert is the Sahara in North Africa.
It is 20 times larger than Britain.

The highest clouds are the cirrus, which are between 6,000 and 10,000 metres up. The lowest, the stratus, are about 1,000 metres up.

The biggest clouds are the cumulo-nimbus, which can grow to 20 kilometres high in the tropics.

The biggest island is Australia: it is really a continent.
It is 28 times bigger than Britain.
Next largest is Greenland.

The largest rivers. By volume of water, the largest river is the Amazon. It is about 6,300 kilometres long, flowing from Peru, across Brazil, to the Atlantic, where its estuary is 80 kilometres wide.
It has many hundreds of tributary rivers, many longer than any in Europe.
By length, the largest is the Nile which flows into the Mediterranean; at over 6,400 kilometres long, it is the only river longer than the Amazon.
In Europe the longest river is the Rhine; it is 1,320 kilometres long.

The deepest part of the ocean is the Marianas Trench in the Pacific.
The bottom of it is 11,034 metres below sea level.

■ The time zones

When you get up to go to school each day, in the United States it is still night-time and people are still asleep. Why isn't it the same time everywhere at once?

Sunrise happens at different times in different places, as they turn to face the Sun. All over the world clocks are set to agree with the timing of day and night for their own area.

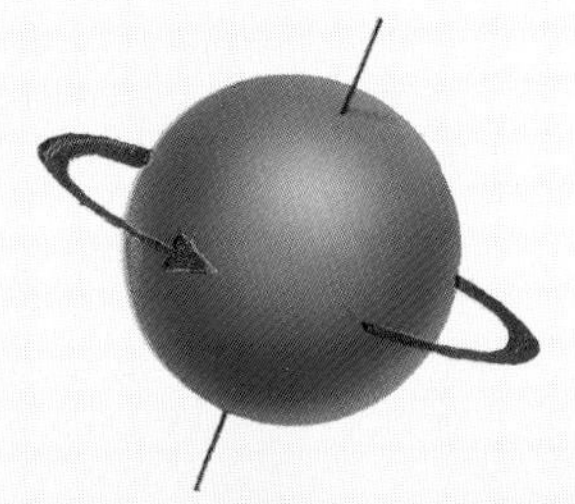

To calculate what time it is in another country, we take a zero point through the meridian at Greenwich in London, and divide the map into 24 zones, one for each hour of the day. Then each time we go from one zone to the next, we change time by one hour.

Between London and Tokyo in Japan, there are 9 time zones, so there is a difference of 9 hours.

Because the Earth spins in a westwards direction, the Sun rises earlier further east. So, as you go east, you need to add on hours to the time. When you go west, you subtract hours. When it is noon in London, it is nine in the evening in Japan, and seven in the morning in New York.

Sometimes, for convenience, a country may decide to alter its official time from what it should be for its time zone. This may be so it can have the same time as the countries next door, making telephone calls easier. France and Spain have decided to have the same time as the rest of continental Europe further east. Only Britain and Portugal have a different time.

Using this map, you can work out for yourself what time it is in any country in the world.

To make the time zones, the Earth is divided into slices, shaped rather like the segments of an orange. **The imaginary lines that separate the segments are the meridians.** Each segment, or piece, is a time zone in which everybody should have the same time. There are twenty-four altogether, just as there are twenty-four hours in a day. This is how long the Earth takes to make one whole turn.

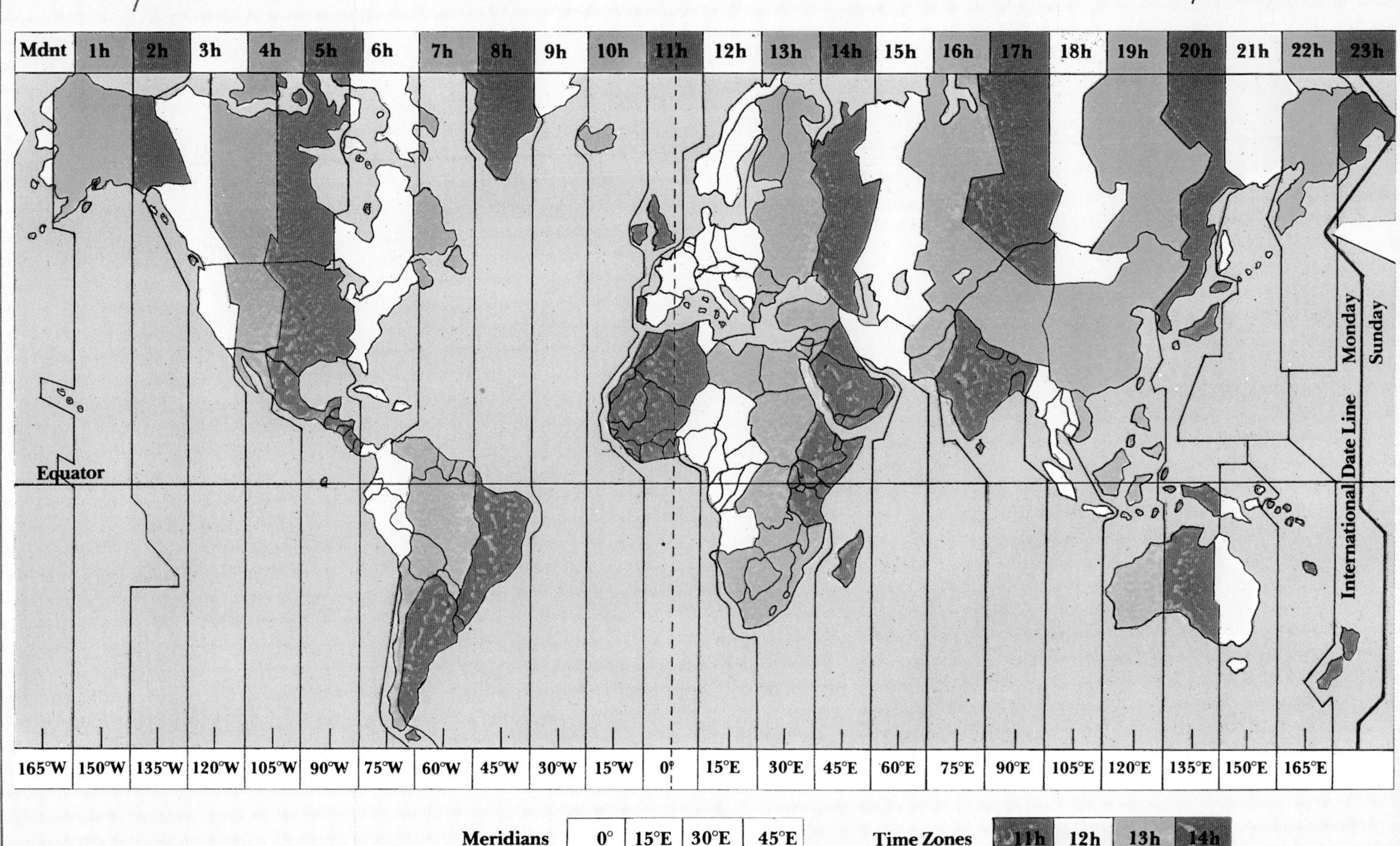

■ What will the weather be like tomorrow?

People who work on the land, or who live in the mountains, or sail the seas, look for all sorts of signs that predict the weather.

Pine cones are very sensitive to dampness in the air. The scales on the cone close up when it is going to rain, and open out in dry weather.

The carline thistle is hung over doorways in France to predict the weather. The thistle opens when the weather is turning fine, and shuts when bad weather threatens.

Animals, too, know when the weather is going to get worse:

Cows lick themselves, **horses** paw the ground and stick their necks out to breathe noisily, while **bees** stay in their hives.

Spiders and frogs are wonderful 'animal barometers'.

If it's going to be wet and stormy, the spider reinforces her web or even makes it smaller, and hides herself away. When it's going to be fine, she spins a bigger web. It'll be a fine, clear night if she does this in the evening.

If you see a frog sitting out on a lawn or field, it means the air is nice and damp for him, and it will soon rain. If he hides away under a stone, then the air is dry, and there is sunshine on the way.

Donkeys shake their ears, and bray continuously.

Flies, mosquitoes and horse-flies bite much more in wet weather.

Butterflies flit close to the windows.

Worms and snails come out into the garden.

People say that **cats** tend to wash behind their ears when the air is moist.

Moles get busy, making their molehills higher.

Hens scratch around, take a dust bath, and collect their chicks together.

■ The giants of astronomy

These are just some of the people who made great discoveries about the skies.

Ptolemy lived in Alexandria in Ancient Egypt. He believed the Earth was the centre of the Universe. For 1,500 years, everybody considered his book on astronomy to be the most important ever written.

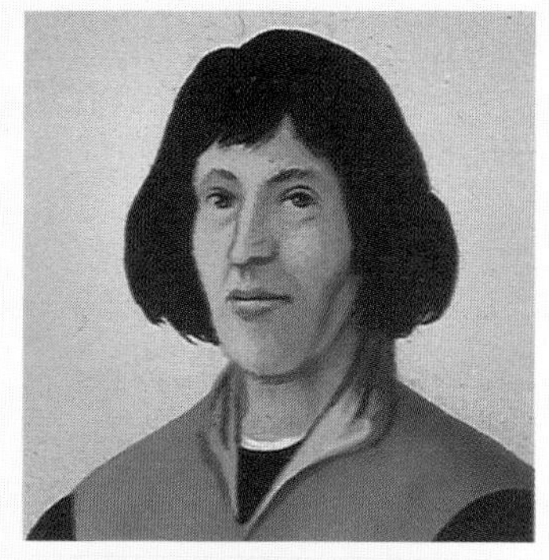

Copernicus (1473–1543) overturned Ptolemy's ideas at last. He showed that the Earth was spinning in space, and that it travelled around the Sun over a year, making it a planet like the others.

Johannes Kepler (1571–1630) showed that the planets don't travel in circles, but make ellipses around the Sun. He explained this through mathematical laws.

■ Quiz

Each question has only one right answer. When you think you have found it, you can check with the answers at the bottom of the next page.

1. How long has the Sun been exploding?
a) 500 million years
b) 5 million years
c) 12 billion years

2. The Moon is . . .
a) bigger than the Earth
b) the same size
c) smaller

3. The equinox is the time when . . .
a) the days are the longest
b) the days are the shortest
c) day and night are of equal length

4. In summer the Earth goes round the Sun . . .
a) more slowly
b) faster
c) at the same speed as the rest of the year

5. The time just before night is called . . .
a) dawn
b) dusk
c) the aurora

6. When it's nine in the morning in London, what time is it in New York?
a) four in the morning
b) eight in the evening
c) three in the afternoon

7. You hear thunder . . .
a) at the same time as you see lightning
b) a few seconds after the lightning
c) just before the lightning

8. The tides are caused by . . .
a) the rotation of the Earth alone
b) the pull of gravity from the Moon
c) the rotation of the Earth around the Sun

9. An iceberg is . . .
a) a piece of pack ice
b) ice broken off a glacier
c) a block of rock covered with ice

10. From one full Moon to the next takes . . .
a) 31 days
b) 27 days
c) 30 days

Galileo Galilei (1564–1642) was the first person to look at the sky through a telescope. He saw things which no one had ever seen before – the moons of Jupiter, and the rings of Saturn.

Newton (1642–1727) was a physicist, mathematician, and astronomer. His law of gravitation explains why an apple falls to the ground, and why the Moon goes on circling the Earth.

Einstein (1879–1955) was probably the greatest scientist of the twentieth century. His theory of relativity completely changed our understanding of the Universe. It was true for very small things like electrons as well as for the whole Universe. He realised that the ordinary laws of physics cannot be applied to objects travelling at the speed of light.

■ People have always dreamt of exploring under the sea!

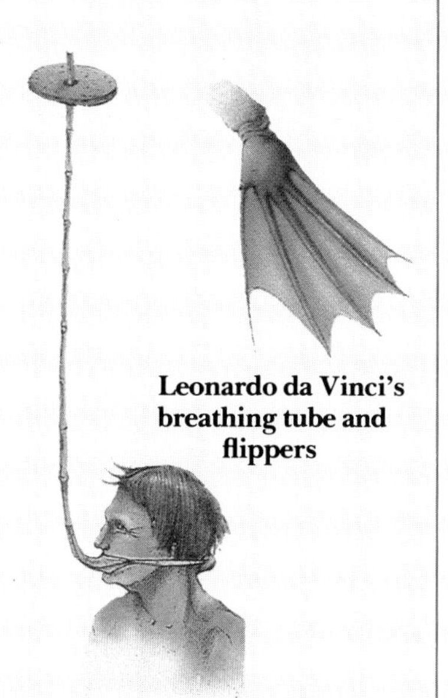

Leonardo da Vinci's breathing tube and flippers

In the 15th century, Leonardo da Vinci, an artist and scientist, designed flippers and a mask with a breathing tube.

■ Quiz

11. Which planet is nearest to the Sun?
a) Venus
b) Mercury
c) The Earth

12. Which planet is furthest from the Sun?
a) Pluto
b) Neptune
c) Uranus

13. We measure atmospheric pressure with ...
a) a barometer
b) a thermometer
c) an anemometer

14. Which colour is on the outside of a rainbow?
a) red
b) yellow
c) indigo

15. A hurricane is a wind of force ...
a) 9
b) 10
c) 12

16. Which ocean is the biggest?
a) the Atlantic
b) the Pacific
c) the Antarctic

17. The Sun rises ...
a) in the east
b) in the south
c) in the west

18. The Earth's neighbour planets are ...
a) Venus and Mars
b) Mercury and Mars
c) Jupiter and Saturn

19. A shooting star is ...
a) a star travelling across the sky
b) the shining trail of a meteorite
c) dust particles from the Sun

20. Atmospheric pressure is ...
a) greatest near the ground
b) greatest on tall mountains
c) the same at all heights

Answers: 1b, 2c, 3c, 4c, 5b, 6a, 7b, 8b, 9b, 10b, 11b, 12a, 13a, 14a, 15c, 16b, 17a, 18a, 19b, 20a

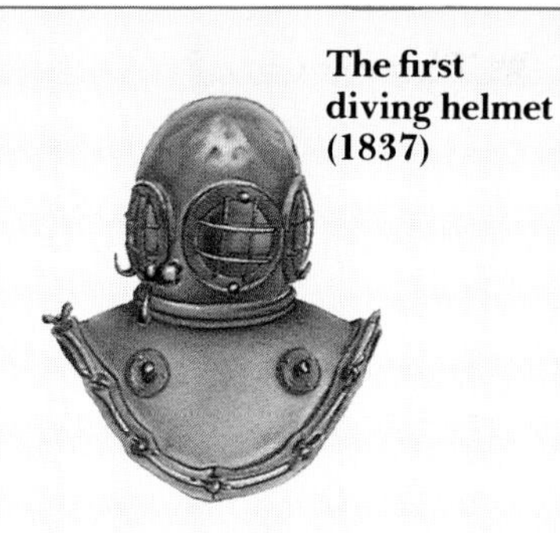

The first diving helmet (1837)

In the 19th century a French writer, Jules Verne, wrote a story about Captain Nemo, who lived 20,000 leagues under the sea. Nemo's submarine was a fabulous palace for watching the creatures of the deep.

In reality, submarine exploration began with diving bells, which allowed a man to go down to 60 metres. Bathyscaphes allowed much greater depths. The first, invented by a Frenchman, Auguste Piccard, went as deep as 1,830 metres, in 1948. In 1960, the present record was reached – 10,916 metres, by the *Trieste*.

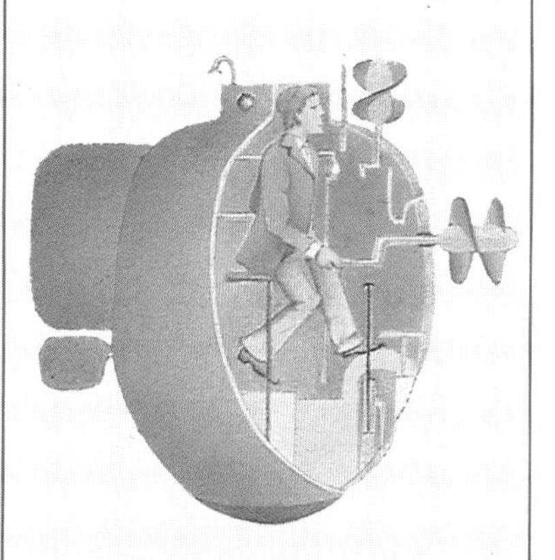

A diving machine (1776)

■ Glossary

Air: the gases and water vapour that make up our atmosphere. The exact proportions of the gases varies, according to temperature, altitude, and pollution.
Antarctica: the ice-covered continent south of latitude 66°S, where the South Pole is.

Arctic: the area around the North Pole, north of latitude 66°N. The region is mostly sea, covered with floating pack ice.
Astrologer: a person who sees a connection between events on the Earth and the positions of the stars and planets.
Astronomer: a person who studies the skies.
Atmosphere: the gases that surround a planet,

held to it by gravity. Earth's atmosphere extends up over 1,000 kilometres.

Bay: a wide curved part of the coastline, where there is a sandy or pebbly beach that curves inwards between two headlands.
Black smoker: a plume of gas coming from inside the Earth on to the deep ocean floor. Black smokers are rich in zinc, lead and other useful metals. Strange creatures live nearby.

Carbon dioxide: a gas that is a small but important part of our air. Mammals breathe it out, and plants absorb it in daylight. It traps the heat radiated from the Earth's surface.
Climate: the usual pattern of weather for a region.
Comet: the word comes from one meaning 'long-haired'. Astronomers use the word for objects that travel through the solar system and have a long shining tail of gas.
Condensation: happens when steam turns to water. This usually occurs when steam touches something cold.
Continent: an area of land thousands of kilometres across, maybe so large it has seas within it. The Earth's oldest rocks are in the continents.
Core of the Earth: the dense metal at the centre of the Earth, consisting mainly of iron. Much of the core is molten, but the centre is thought to be solid.
Crust of the Earth: the outer solid layer of the Earth, about 5 kilometres thick in the oceans, and 35 kilometres thick in the continents.

Degrees Celsius: a measure of how hot or cold something is, named after a Swedish astronomer.
Desert: a region with less than a quarter of a metre of rainfall a year, where plants and animals are very rare.

Eclipse: the time when the light from a star, planet or other object in the sky is blocked by another one passing between you and it.
Epicentre: the point on the surface of the Earth above the place where an earthquake begins.
Equator: an imaginary line around the widest part of a star, moon or planet.
Equinox: the time when day and night are the same length on the Earth.
Erosion: the gradual wearing down of rocks and soil, by wind or water, or other causes.

Evaporation: happens when a liquid turns into a gas, usually because it has been heated.

Galaxy: one of billions of groups of stars, gas and dust in the Universe.
Gravity: the force that pulls things towards the Earth or any other planet.

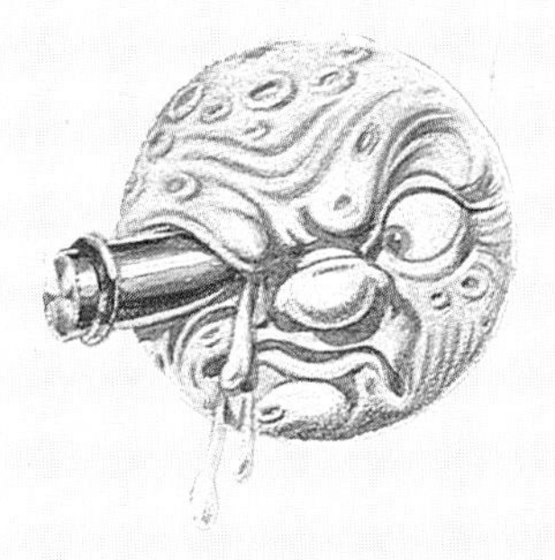

Greenwich meridian: an imaginary line passing through Greenwich, London, on which all the time zones are based.

Hemisphere: the two halves of the planet either side of the Equator. The Earth has a northern, boreal, and a southern, austral, hemisphere.
Horizon: an imaginary line where sky and land meet. Looking out over the sea, it is the line where the sky seems to join the sea.
Hydrogen: a very lightweight gas. It is the lightest chemical element of all.

Ice Age: a time when our climate was colder. The last Ice Age began 3 million years ago, and ended about 10,000 years ago.

Legend: a story which passes from generation to generation, often by storytelling rather than by writing.
Lunar: connected with the Moon.

Mantle of the Earth: the rocky part of the Earth which surrounds the iron core, and is underneath the crust.
Meteorite: a piece of a planet which exploded long ago, and much later fell on to another planet.
Milky Way: the name of our galaxy. You can also call it the Galaxy, with a capital 'G'.
Moisture: a small amount of water turned into gas and mixed into the air.
Month: a calendar month is 30 or 31 days (except for February); a lunar month – one circling of the Earth by the Moon – is about 28 days.
Moon: any ball of rock which orbits around a planet.
Mouth: where a river reaches the sea.

Ocean: the water covered part of the Earth, where the sea bed is made of young volcanic rocks. Much of the surface of the Earth is covered by oceans.
Orbit: the journey a moon, planet, star or galaxy makes around another object in the Universe. The Earth's orbit round the Sun takes a year.
Oxygen: a gas making up about one fifth of the Earth's atmosphere. Almost all forms of life need it to live: we breathe it in the air; fish breathe it in the water. Plants give it out in sunlight.

Pebbles: rounded fragments of rock found on beaches and in rivers.
Phase of the Moon: any one of the shapes of the Moon that we see repeated, such as the crescent, the half or the full Moon.
Plates of the Earth: pieces of the Earth's crust and mantle, which fit together and cover the whole surface of the Earth.
Poles: the most northerly and most southerly parts of the Earth. The line between them is the axis about which the Earth is spinning like a top.

Radar: an electronic instrument using radio waves to locate any moving or fixed object.
Richter: an American scientist who studied how big earthquakes are. We measure earthquakes using the scale he invented.
Rotate: to spin around, as the Earth does around its axis.

Satellite: a small object in the Universe which makes an orbit around another, bigger object. The Moon is a satellite of the Earth. There are also many man-made satellites.
Scatter: to send off in all directions.
Shooting star: a meteorite so small it burns up completely in the Earth's atmosphere. It looks like a fast-moving star in the sky.
Solar flare: a sudden burst of very hot gas from part of the Sun's surface.
Solstice: the summer solstice is midsummer, when the day is longest, and the winter solstice is midwinter, when the day is shortest.
Source: where a river begins.

Tidal surge: an unusually high tide, which happens during a storm when atmospheric pressure is unusually low.

Tropics: the parts of the Earth near the Equator, where the Sun is directly overhead sometime during the year.

Universe: everything that exists; all the millions of stars, planets and moons, as well as energy and space.

Vapour: another name for steam, a cloud of tiny liquid drops.

White dwarf star: the last stage in the life of a

star, when it collapses and becomes very, very dense.

Year: 365 days, the length of time it takes the Earth to make its journey right round the Sun.

Zodiac: the zone of the sky through which we see the Sun, the Moon and all the planets travelling. The groups of stars they seem to travel through are called the signs of the Zodiac. The astrologer uses these patterns to find out what the future holds.

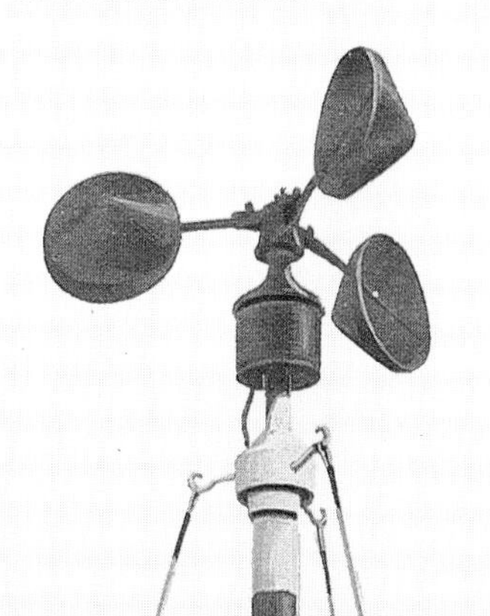

■ Ways of speaking

The Sun

'A place in the Sun' is a good place to be, whether it is really in the sunshine, or where people like and respect you.
'Make hay while the Sun shines' means take the opportunity to do something you want to, while you can.
Do you look on 'the sunny side of things'?

The stars

'To sleep under the stars' is to sleep out of doors.
'To thank your lucky stars' is to say you are grateful for a piece of good luck that came your way.

The Moon

The Latin word for the

Moon is 'luna'. Several words to do with the Moon are based on this.
'Lunatic' (or 'loony' for short) means 'moonstruck'. This used to be a way of saying 'mad'; the Moon was thought to cause madness.
When you say something happens 'once in a blue moon', you mean it happens very, very rarely.
If you are 'over the moon' about something, you are very happy.

Day and night

A person who is really elegant and lovely to look at is said to be 'as beautiful as the day is long'.
'It's as clear as daylight' means I understand exactly what you have said.
'They are like day and night' means two people or things are totally unlike each other.

The seasons

'The spring of your life' is when you are young.
'The autumn of your life' is when you are past middle age.

The sky and the heavens

Saying 'thank heavens!' shows that you are glad and relieved about something.

'To move heaven and earth' to get something done means to do everything you possibly can to make sure it happens.
'When the skies fall' is when there is a terrible disaster.
Someone 'in seventh heaven' is really happy.
'The sky's the limit' means you have the ability to do just about anything, and there is nothing to stop you.

The Earth

'To go to ground' means to go into hiding until something nasty stops happening.
'To come down to Earth' means to stop day-dreaming and get on with doing practical things.

Volcanoes

'Sleeping under a volcano' means taking a big risk. Everything seems safe now, but something awful could happen at any moment.

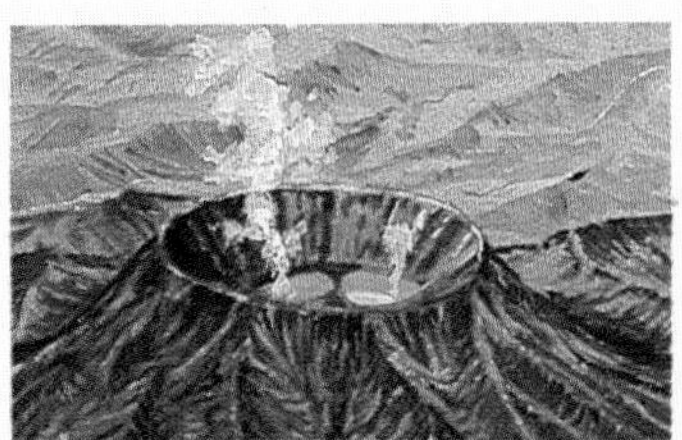

Here is a list of organizations you could join and museums you can visit. Your library will be able to tell you if the local museum has an interesting geology department.

Geologists' Association
Burlington House
Piccadilly
London W1V 9AG

Nationwide Geology Club
13 Acacia Avenue
Chappeltown
Sheffield S30 4PQ

Geological Museum
Exhibition Road
London SW7 2DE

Science Museum
Exhibition Road
London SW7 2DE

The Junior Astronomical Society
36 Fairway
Keyworth
Nottingham NG12 5DU

In Canada:

Canadian Museum of Nature
Education Section
P.O. Box 3443
Station "D"
Ottawa

National Museum of
Science and Technology
Skynews 1
1867 St. Laurent Blvd
P.O. Box 9724
Ottawa Terminal
Ottawa

In Australia:

Australian Museum
College Street
Sydney
(02) 969 2777
[P.O. Box A285]
SYDNEY SOUTH
New South Wales 2000

The entries in **bold** refer to whole chapters on the subject.